EVERYDAY APOLOGETICS

TRAVIS DICKINSON

SEMINARY HILL PRESS

Seminary Hill Press
2001 West Seminary Drive
Fort Worth, Texas 76115

Everyday Apologetics
By Travis Dickinson
Copyright © 2015 by Travis Dickinson
ISBN: 978-0-9839392-6-9
Publication Date: June 2015

TABLE OF CONTENTS

Chapter 1 1

Chapter 2 15

Chapter 3 27

Chapter 4 41

Chapter 5 57

Chapter 6 71

Appendix 1: College Guide 81

Appendix 2: How to get apologetics
at your church 87

1

Apologetics as devotional

Apologetics: commending and defending the truth of Christianity.

Stereotypes are funny things. They are often false and many times offen-
sive, but on the other hand, they can also be well-deserved. Apologetics
has a stereotype, and it often seems well-deserved. Have you ever tried
to read an apologetics text and found yourself wondering what advanced
degree you needed to have just to follow the discussion? We've failed to
deliver apologetics with a broad appeal to our culture because so much of
the material is overly cerebral.

I'm involved in a handful of apologetics conferences throughout the year
and, let's face it, these are not the big-ticket events in the Christian world.
Is this because people don't go to Christian conferences? No way! Living
in the Dallas/Fort Worth area, there are major conferences all throughout
the year. Some of these cost more than a weekend at an all-inclusive resort
in the Caribbean. They are practically stadium-sized, and they often sell
out.

So what's going on? It seems to me that these events target very different
parts of our souls. Many of our big Christian events target the passionate,
emotional part of our souls. This is not a bad thing, as we are passionate,
emotional beings. An apologetics event, by contrast, often targets the rational part of our souls. The problem comes when we value passion over the

rational. Jesus tells us that the greatest commandment is to love God with all of who we are, including our hearts and minds (Matt. 22:37-38). We are to passionately worship God, but this involves our intellects as well as our hearts.

Perhaps you're thinking, "But we shouldn't be overly rationalistic in our faith." I'd be the first to agree. Again, the command is to love God with all of who we are, and so of course we shouldn't neglect our passion and only emphasize the intellect. However, this is hardly an epidemic in the church! It seems to me that we struggle far more often to even show up intellectually in the church.

So, I'd like to confront this stereotype and recast the thing we call *doing apologetics*.

In my view, apologetics should be a very normal part of discipleship unto the Lord Jesus. However, please resist the stereotype that just popped into your head. I'm not saying that you must enroll in an advanced degree or begin reading highly academic books and articles that often swing for the academic fences. In fact, the sort of apologetics I have in mind and that I will recommend could be done by anyone, including children[1] and even someone who lacks the ability to read.

Recasting apologetics

Let's begin with the proper authority: Scripture. Peter says:

> ...but sanctify Christ as Lord in your hearts, always being ready to make a defense to everyone who asks you to give an account for the hope that is in you, yet with gentleness and reverence. (1 Peter 3:15)

This is often the "go to" passage for many apologetics textbooks and presentations, but unfortunately, the context of the passage is rarely highlighted. If we fail to consider the context, we risk missing what Peter is saying. The overall context of the passage is that Peter is describing how to do relationships *Christianly*. He begins chapter 3 by addressing husbands and wives directly and then more broadly speaks to how we are to relate to

---

1 This is not to say that the ensuing discussion has children in mind. Some of it will be challenging. The point is that this approach could be employed by anyone.

others. Then he says:

> To sum up, all of you be harmonious, sympathetic, broth-
> erly, kindhearted, and humble in spirit; not returning evil
> for evil or insult for insult, but giving a blessing instead. (1
> Peter 3:8-9)

As we see in this passage, it is thoroughly Christian to work for harmony
and peace. However, the reality is that it is not always going to work.
Sometimes folks will persecute us precisely for doing good. When this sort
of suffering occurs, Peter tells us that we should not fear the intimidation
and should not be troubled (v. 14). Instead, and here it comes, with Christ
as Lord in our hearts, we are to be ready to make an intellectual defense
(an *apologia*) of the hope—namely, the Gospel—that is within us (v. 15).

The context of this passage is that Peter is detailing how Christians should
relate to others and live in the world. The interesting thing is that he links
having Christ sanctified in our hearts with being ready to make a defense.

There are many things we see in this passage. I will list four observations.

First observation The term Peter uses here, from which we derive the
word "apologetics," is *apologia*. This is a legal term that at least vaguely
resembles what a contemporary lawyer does in a courtroom. The lawyer
not only responds to objections but also asserts positive theses about his or
her client and will *defend* these theses. In short, the lawyer provides reasons
for thinking a certain thesis is true. Similarly, the disciple of Jesus Christ is
called to be ready to provide reasons for thinking that Christianity is true.

Second observation We should notice that Peter is not only addressing
pastors and church leaders. He is characterizing Christians in general. He
begins v. 8 with "all of you." Being ready to defend is not optional. It is for
every Christian everywhere, no matter one's vocation. It is as relevant to
the plumber as it is to the pastor.

Third observation Peter provides us with only one tone in which these
sorts of conversation should take place. When we have opportunity to provide someone the reasons for the hope within, we should do it with gen-
tleness and respect. There will be times in which we can rhetorically win
an argument but lose the battle of winning a soul. This seems to seriously

miss the point, to say the least. When we genuinely respect a lost person as a human being and a seeker, we must gently but firmly make a case for Christianity and gently but firmly point out problems with that person's view. There will be a far greater impact when we approach a conversation in this way.

Fourth observation The thrust of the passage is to be *prepared* to do apologetics as a result of having a sanctified heart. This is not a command to go out and accost the nearest atheist. The call here is not so much to a ministry to others as much as an attitude of the heart and a condition of the mind; to be a certain kind of person first.

This is not to say that apologetics has nothing to do with ministering to others. We are all called to make disciples (Matt. 28:19-20), and this will often involve making a defense of various aspects of the faith. But we often look at apologetics as primarily a ministry to atheists and unbelievers. We may sign up for a study in Christian apologetics to know what to say to our colleague who is vocally hostile to any religious faith or the family members who give everyone a piece of their mind at holidays. This is undoubtedly part of the apologetic enterprise, but it seems to skip to answering the questions of others before we have genuinely asked the questions for ourselves. If someone asked you to give an account for the hope that is in you, what would you say in defense of this position? I find that many people in the church have not thought about what reasons they do, in fact, have. Apologetics should begin by first working out this account for ourselves as the proper source for doing outreach to others.

With this in mind, we see that Peter's call here is in perfect accord with what Jesus identifies as the greatest commandment:

> 'You shall love the Lord your God with all your heart, and with all your soul, and with all your mind.' This is the great and foremost commandment. (Matt. 22:37-38)

As I alluded to above, the church seems to have at least a grasp of what it means to love God with our hearts. We have a community in which we routinely pour out our hearts to God, if we are lucky. Loving God with all of our hearts, no doubt, means a lot more than this, but at the same time, it seems to mean at least this. In any case, we understand what it means to love God with our hearts, and perhaps we know what it means to love God with our souls, but very few of us know what it means to love God with our minds. Peter's call illuminates part of what it means to fulfill this command. We love God with our minds by thinking and being intelligent about the reasons we hope in the Gospel. We avoid the simplistic, "God says it, I believe it, that settles it." This may work as a bumper sticker and is likely well-intentioned, but at the end of the day, it doesn't seem to honor God. Perhaps some of us are content with this slogan, but I have found that many people are curious enough to ask, "Did God actually say it?" and, "Why should I believe it is true?" and, "Why think a catchy slogan should settle anything?" These seem like fair questions for all of us to ask, and our ability to answer them is the objective of apologetics.

Loving God with our minds

How do we become prepared to give a defense of our Christian faith? This, I think, should start with intellectual curiosity. We ought to love God with our minds by embracing an intellectual pursuit of God and by recognizing our faith as an important part of our discipleship.

Unfortunately, over the course of the last century, Christians have progressively moved away from approaching God intellectually. As a result, the church is no longer biblically and theologically literate. These days, it seems that slogans have taken the place of careful thought about a Christian worldview. However, there are intellectual challenges that are having their way with our children and with those who are less mature in the faith. Slogans and emotional fervor simply do not meet these challenges. They require the hard work of making subtle distinctions and crafting carefully worked-out arguments. But it is often thought that this is primarily the work of the pastor or the Christian academic. As we saw in 1 Peter 3:15, however, being prepared to give a defense is a requirement for every Christian. No exceptions.

In 2 Corinthians 10:4, Paul describes the work of the Christ-follower as being, in part, one who tears down fortresses. What sort of fortresses does Paul have in mind? He clarifies in v. 5, saying, "We are destroying speculations and every lofty thing raised up against the knowledge of God, and we are taking every thought captive to the obedience of Christ." The fortresses are largely intellectual. J.P. Moreland said, "Spiritual warfare is largely, though not entirely, a war of ideas, and we fight bad, false ideas with better ones."[2] So how does one destroy ideas and speculations? They must be refuted. But to fulfill this call, we must employ the tools and skills of critical thinking that will not come simply by sitting through a Sunday morning church service, no matter how intellectually challenging that may be.

So, as Christians, we need to be interested in cultivating and developing our minds. Here are a few suggestions to begin cultivating the life of the mind.

First, in order for our Christian worldview to survive our culture as we encounter ideas, we have to become active rather than passive thinkers. Ideally, we would never embrace an idea without making a conscious choice to do so. G.K. Chesterton once said, "An open mind is really a mark of foolishness, like an open mouth. Mouths and minds were made to shut; they were made to open only in order to shut."[3] This can be hard work, but keeping ideas out that are contrary to the knowledge of God is practically impossible if we absorb the ideas around us uncritically and without noticing.[4]

Second, if we are to recognize ideas that are contrary to the knowledge of God, we need to know Scripture and Christian theology. Otherwise, we won't know if the idea is contrary or not. We need to value and devote ourselves to rigorous study of Scripture and theology, both individually and in our churches. If we are not well-grounded in our own worldview and do not have an anchor point from which we can then evaluate objections and competing views, then we'll never succeed in this.

---

2   This quote comes from the series preface entitled "A Call to Integration" that is in each volume for IVP *Christian Worldview Integration Series*. Moreland also details thoughts about how to confront ideas in a culture in *Love Your God with All Your Mind: The Role of Reason in the Life of the Soul* (Colorado Springs, CO: NavPress, 2012), chapter 6.

3   Chesterton, G.K. "The Best Critic" *Illustrated London News*. October 10, 1908.

4   This is especially important when it comes to children. We need to resist the temptation to plop our kids down in front of the TV or tablet to watch and absorb whatever they fancy. I'm not saying that kids shouldn't consume media, but unless we teach our kids to think critically about what they watch, they will tend absorb these ideas uncritically. I suggest watching the movie or show together and talking about it afterwards. This can be a lot of fun, because kids like to talk about their favorite movies and shows.

Third, we must value *thinking well*. This may seem obvious, but when we examine what sort of care we take with how we think, it reveals that there is not a high value placed on the life of the mind. This is going to look very different for people depending on where they are on this journey. In my view, we should aim to achieve the highest level of intellectual study feasible in our current context. We live in a day and age when increasing our intellectual abilities has never been easier. There is a growing library of books and curricula that can meet you wherever you are. There are a great number of apologetic ministries, many of which have very informative websites. An unimaginable number of hours of online lectures and debates are available as a free download online. There are even a number of smart phone apps devoted to apologetics.

Asking the deep and difficult questions

As we grow in our intellectual pursuit of God, we ought to begin a practice that can be quite intimidating. As we are ready for it, we should start to honestly wrestle with the case for Christianity, including positive reasons for Christianity and the ideas that challenge the truth of Christianity. I recommend starting slowly and enlisting the help of others who are further along in this regard.

We often wait to ask deep and difficult questions until we are on the precipice of a crisis. Perhaps our teenage child is considering leaving the faith due to some questions that have, in his or her mind, only received pat answers. Because we love our child, we suddenly have an interest in asking these questions. Unfortunately, this can sometimes be too late. Or we may have a co-worker creating a hostile work environment by badgering us about our faith. After being left speechless and looking stupid, we are only now interested in considering these matters for ourselves.

A sampling of the sort of deep and difficult questions I have in mind:

- Why think that God exists?
- Why does God allow so much evil in the world?
- How could a loving God deal so severely with various people groups in the Old Testament?
- Why think that Scripture is true and accurate?

- Are there contradictions in Scripture?

- Did Jesus really rise from the dead?

- Can I believe in miracles?

- Is science in conflict with faith?

We are not trying to formulate answers to these questions merely to confront the skeptic; we ask these questions for ourselves precisely because they are interesting questions. It seems to me we should be curious about these things if we have not had occasion to think about them before.

Now, we need to ask these questions for ourselves, but we should never pursue them by ourselves. What I mean is that we should individually be thinking about these things, but we are not alone in this. Doing this in community is essential to doing this well. We need to find like-minded brothers and sisters in Christ who can walk this journey with us. Like so many things in life, when it comes to intellectual progress, we can do far more together than we can alone.

We also need mentors. We need to have others who are further along in this journey to whom we can go when going gets tough. It's amazing what a good mentor can help us solve when we have ourselves all tied up in intellectual knots. We also need mentors from a distance. These are intellectual mentors whom you may not ever have the privilege of meeting, but you sit under them through their writing. These may even be folks who have passed away long ago but have left a legacy of intellectual thought.

Questioning God?

What may be a worry at this point is that it might sound like I'm recommending we adopt a spirit of skepticism and cynicism, never satisfied with the plain teachings of Scripture. The thought may arise that we are called to a childlike faith, not this skeptical posture. This is an important objection, and one that I take very seriously, because I do not think that the apologetic call is for us to become cynical and doubting. Many well-meaning Christian philosophers have pushed students to question their faith too hard without ever teaching students how to question well. This can result in the student walking away from his or her faith in confusion. I am definitely not aiming here at confusion. Rather, I'm aiming at genuinely knowing God more fully through pursuing him intellectually.

Children are a great example for us. It is important to note that the call to *childlike* faith is not a call to *childish* faith. In fact, the writer of Hebrews challenges us to leave behind childish thinking about God—the milk—and dine in maturity on solid food (Heb. 6:1-2). Jesus points us to the quality of being childlike on more than one occasion. Children have an almost undying trust and faith in the adults in their lives.

Now it's true that children are very trusting, but they are also VERY curious, and many children beautifully strike the balance between trust and curiosity. They ask questions, questions, and more questions. One of my children is especially given to curiosity. She asks questions about EVERYTHING! I sometimes have to cut her off, giving her the "Okay sweetie, last question," because if I don't, I won't make it to work on time. However, in all of these questions, I have never once felt that she didn't trust me. In fact, she comes to me with questions precisely because she trusts me and loves me. When children ask questions, their attitude is rarely skeptical or cynical (that comes later in the teen years). Generally speaking, they are not trying to usurp or unseat the authority of their father or mother. They are just simply and intensely curious. My daughter may ask me, "How does a car make us go so fast?" because she is filled with wonder and awe at moving down the highway. She doesn't hesitate to get in the car with me and is not in any way cynical about it. She is simply voicing a puzzle to someone who is an authority to her, an authority whom she loves.

Another example is of those who are newly and wildly in love. It is possible for these lovers to gaze into each other's eyes and simply study one another. In fresh, new love, we want to know everything there is to know about our significant other. We want to know how he/she thinks and are intrigued by minor details of response. This is not because we don't trust our new love. In fact, we probably trust him/her to a fault. But we have an insatiable curiosity. A woman experiencing such a love would never be satisfied with the statement, "He says it, I believe it, that settles it." Instead, out of a deep, loving curiosity, she would want to know why he says it.

Allow me a final illustration that many students and I have found useful. I routinely fly on airplanes, and many of you reading this do, too. Quite regularly, we literally entrust our lives to—indeed, place our faith in—these airplanes. However, I know next to nothing about flight. Somehow, this craft composed primarily of steel weighing in at around 1 million pounds can lift off the ground and ascend to 30,000 feet in the sky and get us to our destination. If we let this sink in, it is wondrously amazing. It is very natural for us to have a question (or thirty) out of curiosity regarding how this is even possible. But notice that we can have these questions and still make our flight to Chicago or Los Angeles. We can maintain our questions and most likely have many of them go unanswered. We can ask how a million pounds of mostly steel can soar through the air, 6 miles up, and all the while *continue to trust the airplane*. In fact, we can even have a friendly conversation about aeronautics while in the air if we have the good fortune to sit next to someone who knows about these things. I may not understand a lick of it, but we can finish our conversation and go on our merry way once the plane touches down. Notice we need not be skeptics and doubters to be curious about an object of wonder. We can question something in genuine curiosity while still placing faith in the very object of curiosity.

When it comes to God, the call here is to pursue him with curiosity simply as a matter of our love and devotion to him. We can maintain our faith in God while asking deep and difficult questions about our faith, especially when the questioning comes from a deep and abiding love for God and a desire to know him more deeply. With this sort of posture, we don't risk folks losing their faith. Rather, we are set on a journey to know Truth in a deep and abiding way.

What about unbelievers?

We should notice that, with this approach, I have said almost nothing about engaging atheists and non-Christians in arguments and debate; what I have recommended is much more like a devotional exercise. So what about the unbelievers? If we will do this devotional work, when asked by unbelievers to give an account for the hope within, our answers will flow powerfully from this source. For example, if you have thoughtfully engaged these deep and difficult questions, then when you are asked or challenged, you will be a powerful voice to those whose faith is stuck on those questions. It can be incredibly disarming to a person when it is clear that you have deeply wrestled with a question that you are being asked. People don't want textbook answers. If they are thoughtful, they want to see that you are, too.

The discipline of apologetics

We are now in a position to see how this all works out in the broader discipline of apologetics. Apologetics, in its most basic sense, is commending and defending the truth claims of Christianity. This is good, but it is not quite precise enough. Something is marked as apologetic material when the defense doesn't assume anything about Christianity and its sources. That is, we are generally not doing apologetics if we are merely citing Scripture passages as a defense of a claim. A more precise understanding of apologetics is:

> *Commending and defending the truth claims of Christianity without making assumptions that an unbeliever cannot make.*

In other words, when doing apologetics, we are making a case for Christianity that should be compelling to anybody, regardless of a person's view of Scripture or Christianity as a whole. When the theologian defends the doctrine of the Trinity, the theologian will most often do so by showing the doctrine to be pervasively inherent in Scripture.[5] Though this is a defense of a truth claim in Christianity, it would not constitute doing apologetics. The only person who would be persuaded by this is someone who already believes Scripture to be an authoritative source. This would be theology, which is a worthy pursuit indeed. But a question falls within the scope of apologetics when the answer doesn't crucially depend upon these Christian assumptions.

I want to suggest that the primary division in the discipline of apologetics is between *devotional* as opposed to use in *outreach* (i.e., using apologetics to minister to others). I have sketched a picture of the devotional use of apologetics and argued that it is the proper starting place for the use of apologetics in outreach. The outreach use of apologetics can be divided further. On one side, apologetics can be used as a tool in evangelism. This is when we address unbelievers' objections and make a case for the truth of Christianity (more on this in chapter 6). But sometimes believers have questions, too, and these questions can turn into intellectual doubts that

---

5   There are interesting ways in which the Trinity can be defended philosophically without appeal to Scripture. For example, if God is, by definition, perfect, then it is difficult to see how God can be in a relationship with humans without gaining something he lacked. However, in a Trinitarian view, God is in perfect love relationship from all eternity and thus does not gain something he lacks once he enters into relationship with humans.

can be quite debilitating. Therefore, the other side of outreach apologetics is discipleship, whereby apologetics is used to minister to believers' intellectual doubts. This can be quite valuable and helpful.

The following summarizes the breakdown of these various uses of apologetics:

> Apologetics: *Commending and defending the truth claims of Christianity without making assumptions that an unbeliever cannot make.*
>
> A. Devotional Apologetics: pursuing God intellectually out of loving curiosity by asking deep and difficult questions about the faith (this is the proper base for doing outreach apologetics).
>
> B. Outreach Apologetics: engaging others with apologetic material to address objections and make a positive case for Christianity.
>
> > i. Evangelistic apologetics: ministering apologetics to unbelievers.
> >
> > ii. Discipleship apologetics: ministering apologetics to believers, especially those who have doubts.

Conclusion

Do you have questions? If you don't have a few questions about God, then I wonder what sort of view you have of God. Is your view of God a nice, neat, sanitized God? It seems to me that the God of the Bible does not afford us the luxury of putting him in nice, neat boxes. This isn't to say that he is wholly mysterious and that we can't do theology. God has revealed himself to us, and we can know him and know a lot about him. But we are finite and limited. Being perplexed from time to time therefore seems quite appropriate. This, by the way, puts us in good company. Consider the disciples. These were men chosen by Jesus himself and entrusted with the propagation of the church. However, right up to the time of Jesus' ascension, the disciples still didn't really get it. Sure, they trusted Jesus and seemed to be genuinely willing to go wherever and do whatever they were called to do. But they had questions. "Lord, is it at this time You are restoring the kingdom to Israel?" (Acts 1:6). It seems to me that we should be very cautious if we think we have God all figured out.

Now here's the thing: we may be intimidated by this pursuit or even a bit nervous that it will cause us to struggle. In my apologetics classes, I typically have my students investigate through research an objection to Christianity, with the caveat that it can't be a "softball" objection that is easily answered. I have had quite a few students confess that they were nervous about the assignment since they did not want to struggle with doubts. However, every single person who has ever voiced this concern has ultimately concluded that the concern was ill-founded. This is because the resources for Christianity are simply stunning. The tragedy is that most Christians have not availed themselves of these resources.

It's true that some of these resources are too technical for a person who is just beginning this journey. The important thing is that we begin to pursue God intellectually at whatever level we find ourselves. As I said above, this approach is something a child can do. But a child is going to begin in age-appropriate ways. Likewise, you should begin where you are. This is meant to be a lifetime journey of *Everyday Apologetics*, and it is the process that is important. Fall deeply in love with God as you pursue him with your mind.

Reasonable Faith

Faith is the great cop-out, the great excuse to evade the need to think and evaluate evidence. Faith is belief in spite of, even perhaps because of, the lack of evidence. -Richard Dawkins

Before moving on to talk about the specific reasons for faith, it is important that we confront a very common way to talk about faith that ends up cutting the legs out of devotionally loving God with our minds.

Not long ago, a cable TV show host who is an outspoken atheist had on his show a relatively well-known Christian pastor. In a discussion about morality and faith, the host asked the pastor a question about the value of faith. Now to ask a man *of faith* about the value of faith is certainly not out of bounds. But there were two problems with his line of questioning. The first is a general point. The question implies that the pastor has faith and that the TV host does not. This, as we'll see below, is entirely misguided. The TV host, in fact, has faith in many things despite his lack of faith in God. The second point is that the particular way in which the question was asked was unfair. Here is how the question was posed:

"Why is faith good? Why is the purposeful suspension of critical thinking a good thing?"

This, of course, is a leading question, since the host is attempting to force the pastor to answer the first question in light of the definition found in the second. It can be difficult to give a straightforward answer to these sorts of questions since we may have to disentangle the questions before we can answer them.

It was unfair, but really it was only *sort of* unfair, given the way many Christians talk about faith. Many Christians seem quite happy to talk about faith as if it were in some way incompatible with *reason*. For many Christians, there seem to be things we know via science, evidence, and reason, and then there are things we know by faith. We know by reason and evidence that the sun is center of the solar system, how to fix an automobile, and how to do our taxes, but when it comes to knowing that God exists and that Christianity is true, this, some believe, can be known only by faith. We'll refer to this view as *fideism*.

Fideism comes in two basic versions. Let's call the first *moderate fideism*. The prevailing thought in moderate fideism is that reason plays a role, but it can only carry us so far. Sure, we might know some truths of Christianity with reason and evidence, but at a certain point, reason and evidence run out, and faith, in a way, takes over or fills the gap. When it comes to challenges to the faith, the moderate fideist can always appeal to this gap in order to shut down the challenge. At a certain point, the moderate fideist might say, "We just have to have faith."

A second form is what we'll call *strong fideism*. Here you have your rational pursuits on one hand (science, political platforms, home repair, etc.) and your faith pursuits on the other, and never the twain shall meet. Reason and faith are completely distinct pursuits. If this is how one understands faith, then evidence against (or for) the claims of Christianity is largely irrelevant since evidence has nothing to do with faith.

When faith is presented as a contrast to evidence and reason, this seems to suggest that faith is something very much like the purposeful suspension of critical thinking, as the TV host asserted.

I think that both forms of fideism are a mistake. They may, in a certain sense, protect our faith from challenges of reason, but they also prevent the proper and appropriate use of reason in service of our faith. If our Christianity is disconnected from reason, then this makes it impossible to do apologetics (as well as theology, evangelism, and Bible study). Imagine trying to defend a position without being able to use any reasons. How would you even do it? In my view, it is a very serious mistake to think of faith as beyond reason or not relevant to reason. However, to see this, we need to clarify our terms. As we shall see, the only reason to reject reason's relevance to faith is if we have an unnecessarily narrow view of reason.

A reason for reason

I'm afraid that reason gets a bad rap due to the fact that we often have in mind something like academic and formal reasoning (just imagine what a professor might put up on a board with premises and a conclusion). The point is often made that almost no one comes to faith by looking at formal arguments.

I couldn't agree more! I'd be the first to admit that academic and formal reasoning tends to be impractical, and indeed no one comes to faith only from investigating formal arguments. But why think academic formalism is all there is when we refer to "reason"? Notice that when we decide what we'll feed our toddlers, we don't formalize an argument; when we figure out our taxes, we don't formalize arguments; when we problem-solve in the work place, we don't formalize any arguments. And yet all of these are rational pursuits.

The obvious truth is that reasoning does not require formalization. If it did, you wouldn't last long. If you find yourself standing in the way of oncoming traffic, please don't try to formalize an argument before stepping aside! The sight of oncoming traffic should be reason enough. And this is precisely the point. We reason *on the fly*, we do it fast and loose, and we do this almost all the time! One rarely pauses to formalize even when one has advanced degrees in formal logic. It would be a strange person indeed who uses formal logic to decide what he will do with his evening (and whatever it is, he'll likely be doing it alone!).

This is not to say that there aren't important considerations of critical reasoning to keep in mind as we make decisions about life. Indeed, we spent time in chapter 1 talking about how we, as Christians, ought to cultivate the life of the mind. Much of this is learning not just what to think but how to think well, and formal reasoning can be very helpful in this regard. But the point is that when we are deciding what to believe, we often look around at a galaxy of experiences, reports of others (including personal conversations and books), and our own reflections, and from this we settle on a belief that is more or less rational.

So what, then, is reason? For our purposes, we should understand "reason" as any fact (e.g., experiences, testimonies, arguments, reflections, etc.) that seems to indicate the truth of a belief. Let's say someone tells me that the sun is the center of our solar system, and I believe this on the basis of that testimony. Is this reason-based? Of course it is. It is based on the testimonial reason that seems to indicate the truth of the belief. A more important question is whether the belief is rational in the sense that it is based on *good* reason. When it comes to testimony, everything depends on the source of the testimony. If it is a teacher I know to be educated and who has proven generally reliable in the past when it comes to claims such as these, then this is a rational belief. If it is a high school dropout who always consults his magic 8 ball for every question, then this is not a rational belief (despite the fact that it is true).

The point is that it is actually very rare, if even possible, for a belief to be utterly reasonless. We sometimes base our beliefs on less than stellar reasons. For example, we've probably all been guilty of being persuaded by someone who is what I call a *slick talker* and bought trinkets that worked no more than three times. We will even turn over our hard-earned money to someone who is claiming to have the quick fix to all of our financial concerns. We come to trust the salesperson. Do we do this with a reason? Of course. The salesman made it sound like a good deal, and this made it *seem* like it was a good deal. Is it a good reason? If we are honest, no, it probably is not.

Here are some things that I believe:

"Pizza, in general, tastes good."

"My spouse is unswervingly faithful to me."

"Universal rights are a great civil good."

"God raised Jesus from the dead."

I think I have good reasons to believe each of these, though I might have to think through what my specific reasons are in articulating them. I believe in the general tastiness of pizza from a wide variety of experiences with pizza. My belief that my spouse has been faithful to me is also on the basis of a wide variety of experiences, but there is also a track record that continues to improve the rationale of this belief. My guess is that most Americans believe universal rights are a civil good, but it would probably take some digging to discover what reasons we have for thinking so. We might begin reflecting on formal arguments in political philosophy to help us think through these issues.

Now, what about Jesus' resurrection? For most of us, our reason is that the Gospels, as reliable witnesses, affirm the truth of his resurrection. However, just because I use Scripture to justify my position doesn't mean that this is somehow a less reliable use of reason.

To see how this relates to Christian faith more broadly, let's consider an example of a faithful follower of Jesus who happens to lack any formal education. Let's imagine a little, old country grandma who has faithfully served Christ for her whole life despite the fact that she has a limited education. Let's say she obtained the basic skills provided in elementary school but never went further than that. Could her Christian faith possibly be rational? I have met too many country grandmas to doubt that it could be. The country grandma, just like the rest of us, can look around the world and see that the world testifies to God's existence. If she has made specific prayer requests to God, and God showed up in big ways (as he tends to do with the prayers of country grandmas), this would stand as a stellar reason for her Christian faith. The country grandma can have real and powerful encounters with the risen Christ and can experience the realness and power of the Gospel. All of these things are reasons for taking Christianity as true and trustworthy (we'll have more to say about this subject in chapters 4 and 5). Even if she couldn't articulate these reasons, it doesn't follow that they aren't informing her faith.

It seems to me that most committed Christians have a fairly wide repertoire of solid reasons for their faith. This isn't to say that they can't work on making these reasons stronger, but there is no real need to shy away from reason so long as we appropriately expand the scope of reason to include Scripture and the ways in which God works in our lives.

Biblical Faith

With our understanding of "reason" sufficiently broadened, I want to make the claim that to think reason either runs contrary to faith or floats freely apart from faith, or that faith is an otherwise blind, reasonless pursuit, is not biblical.

I have often challenged my students, as something of a homework assignment, to come up with one example from Scripture of so-called "blind faith," where the example illustrates that faith lacks reasons. I goad them a bit by saying I don't think they will find even one instance … but, hey, good luck trying. There is typically at least one enthusiastic student who cannot wait for the next time our class meets and will offer a narrative such as Genesis 22:1-19, wherein Abraham offers up Isaac as a sacrifice, as an example of blind faith. The thought seems to be that Abraham had all the reason in the world not to go through with the sacrifice. After all, this was the child through whom God said he would create a nation. However, despite the reasons, Abraham chose to blindly place his faith in God.

Is it true to say that Abraham had no reason at all?

It seems to me that Abraham made a *very* rational choice. We should keep in mind that God spoke verbally to Abraham and told him (give that one a second) to sacrifice his son. By this time, Abraham had come to believe (for good reasons!) that God is the one and only Almighty God. It wasn't long before this event that Abraham and Sarah conceived Isaac. Of course, every child is a miracle, but it is on a whole different level when Abraham is 100 years old and Sarah is in her early 90s! This undoubtedly had an impact on Abraham's understanding of what God is able to do, and, even more importantly, it expanded his understanding that God is steadfastly faithful to fulfill his covenant promise. In a word, God proved himself to Abraham to be trustworthy, or what we may call *faith-worthy* (more on this notion in a moment). With all of this as backdrop, when the Almighty God of the universe shakes the sound waves and tells you to do something, is it not eminently rational to act accordingly? It's true that he had some competing reasons, but they pale in comparison to the reasons he had for going through with the sacrifice.

This is not unlike Peter's cognitive situation on the Sea of Galilee. In Matthew 14:25-32, Peter demonstrates his faith in the person and power of Jesus by jumping out of a perfectly good boat and, as a result, Jesus enables him to walk on water. But Peter starts looking around at some competing reasons that suggest walking on the water in a violent storm is not such a good idea, and he quickly cedes his trust away from Christ. It is not as if Peter lacked reasons for trusting Christ given all that Peter had seen and come to believe about him. His doubt was the irrational choice. So rather than serve as examples of blind faith, these two biblical accounts nicely illustrate the notion of reasonable faith (or lack thereof, as it turns out for Peter).

Let's look at another passage that some have taken as a commendation of blind faith.

> But Thomas, one of the twelve, called Didymus, was not with them when Jesus came. So the other disciples were saying to him, "We have seen the Lord!" But he said to them, "Unless I see in His hands the imprint of the nails, and put my finger into the place of the nails, and put my hand into His side, I will not believe." After eight days His disciples were again inside, and Thomas with them. Jesus came, the doors having been shut, and stood in their midst and said, "Peace be with you." Then He said to Thomas, "Reach here with your finger, and see My hands; and reach here your hand and put it into My side; and do not be unbelieving, but believing." Thomas answered and said to Him, "My Lord and my God!" Jesus said to him, "Because you have seen Me, have you believed? Blessed *are* they who did not see, and yet believed." (John 20:24-29)

The other disciples tell Thomas that Jesus had risen from the dead. They knew this for a very specific reason: they *saw* the risen Christ. Thomas claims that he will not believe Christ has risen from the dead until he possesses the same reason as they and more still. He wants to not only see Christ but to *touch* his wounds, as well. Though Jesus generously meets this very bold demand, Jesus surely arrests his attention by saying, "Because you have seen me, you have believed," and offers a blessing for those who believe without the evidence of the senses.

Is this a call to blind faith, as it is sometimes taken? It seems to me that to think so would be to go beyond the scope of the blessing here in this text, since the blessing is not given for those who believe blindly with no evidence whatsoever. The blessing is only for those who do not require direct sense experience for belief (those "who have not seen"). But seeing, of course, is not the only way to have evidence and reason for a belief. It is also important to point out that, even without seeing, Thomas already had good reasons for believing. Jesus, who had proven himself to be trustworthy many times over, had predicted his resurrection (Matt. 20:17-19), and Thomas' closest friends testified to him that this had indeed happened. Despite all of this, Thomas wanted more. The blessing that Jesus offers here is not for blind faith but for those who do not demand excessive amounts of evidence (and especially empirical evidence) before they will believe. Good evidence should be good enough.

The mistake Thomas made was that he wanted to have all the details of the situation there before him, without which he would not assent. Remember that he was not just jealous of what the other disciples had in terms of evidence; he demanded details far beyond the threshold of rational belief. He wanted not just to see the risen Savior but also to place his fingers inside of Jesus' wounds.

Like Thomas, we often fall prey to the same temptation to have all the details before us. So often, we want to see the end from the beginning before we will trust God in action. I have spoken to a lot of students who have begun their college training quite sure that they are called to ministry but without a specific idea of where in ministry God will have them. This is sometimes a really tough place to be. We often want to know not only where we are going to be but also how it will turn out and what sacrifices and trouble will we have to confront.

Hebrews 11:1 tells us that biblical faith is the assurance of things *hoped for* and the conviction of things *not seen*. The reality is that the call of God on our lives is something that we look forward to, and many, if not most, of the details are ones of which we are not yet aware. Crucial to biblical faith is maintaining our trust in God despite the fact that we do not get to see the end from the beginning and we may be facing difficult circumstances. God, of course, *could* spell it all out for us, but he typically does not. Oftentimes, we know what we are supposed to be doing now, but that may be it. Why does God keep us on a "need to know" basis about his plans and intentions for us?

To answer this question, let's think about the nature of faith itself. Faith, in my view, is rather simple. Faith is active trust. We trust a lot of things in life. You routinely trust chairs to hold you up, houses and buildings to not fall on your head, airplanes not to fall out of the sky, etc. We should notice that faith always has an object. That is, when you trust, there is always some thing or person in which you put your trust. When you sit in your chair or board an airplane, the object of your trust is the chair or the airplane.

I want to suggest that when we demand complete knowledge of our circumstances and God's plan for us, the object of our trust actually ceases to be God. The object of our faith becomes ourselves and our own abilities, and we decide whether we want to go through with something or not only when God reveals the details. If I were to tell my daughter to hop in the car to go for a ride, and she refused to do so until I told her where we were going, then she wouldn't trust me. When Thomas makes the demand to see and touch the risen Christ, the object of his trust shifts from Christ himself to his own senses. By contrast, when Abraham proceeds to offer up Isaac, Abraham maintains God as the object of his trust, even in something as terrifying as being asked to sacrifice his own child. Abraham didn't know just how this was going to go, and yet he trusted. Hebrews 11:19 tells us that Abraham knew God could raise Isaac from the dead. Notice Abraham's reasoning here doesn't diminish his faith at all. It is for this that he is commended. So it seems to me that at least one reason God does not reveal to us the end from the beginning in all cases is that he wants to be the object of our faith.

Does this elevate reason above faith? No, because these are very different things. One of them is not "over" the other. The whole point is to have faith. But we have to know in what object to place our faith. I think of the relation between faith and reason as one where reason, as a tool, can provide support for our faith. The fact is we can sometimes place our faith or trust in things that turn out to be poorly conceived ideas. Many people have trusted politicians, investments, their own abilities, loved ones, advertising campaigns, etc., for less than compelling reasons and have corresponding horror stories as a result. Though it is certainly not infallible, reason helps us decide which objects are trustworthy, or what we may call *faith-worthy*.

Does this mean that faith is our choice and not a gift of God? Actually, no, but I do not have the space to give this a full treatment. Let me just say that God is the author of our faith by providing reasons for us to believe. God was, in many ways, generous to Abraham. It seems that Abraham couldn't responsibly turn his back on what God had done in his life. Faith was the natural result of God's dealing with him.

I have to say that this is my testimony as well. At this point, it would simply be foolish for me to say there is no God or to trust in my own abilities, as my life can be characterized by a long series of demonstrations of the faithfulness and trustworthiness and realness of God, despite my occasional penchant for ceding my trust to my own self and other things. God, in his grace, has accomplished this in my life.

The atheist's reason for reason

As I noted above, unfortunately, Christians sometimes distance themselves from reason. At the same time, it is very common for atheists to consider reason to be the exclusive right of atheism. This is especially true in a somewhat recent phenomenon known as the New Atheism movement, led by the likes of Richard Dawkins, (the late) Christopher Hitchens, and Sam Harris. There is nothing that is actually "new" about their atheistic beliefs. The only thing that is somewhat novel is their tone and activism.[6] To the New Atheist, faith is, by definition, a suspension of critical thinking, and that's what religious folk trade in. The atheist, however, has no place for faith; atheists rely only upon reason, or so they allege.

This emphasis on reason has become the dominant theme of the New Atheists. In 2012, the "Reason Rally" was held in Washington, D.C. The event featured everyone from Richard Dawkins to Bill Maher to Michael Shermer. It was a who's who of popular-level atheism united around the common theme of reason. This theme shows up routinely in atheist groups. Richard Dawkins has the *Richard Dawkins Foundation for Reason and*

---

6   See, for example, a recent book called *A Manual for Creating Atheists* by Peter Boghossian (Durham, NC: Pitchstone Publishing, 2013).

Science. At one point, if you contributed a significant amount of money to his foundation, you actually got to join the "Reason Circle." There is also the *United Coalition of Reason*, and many other atheist groups lay claim to this theme of reason, as well. Not long ago, there was a lawsuit against the city of Warren, Michigan, due to the fact that the city had denied a petition to put up what was to be called a "Reason Station" by an atheist group. The Reason Station was to be a contrast to a long-standing tradition of having a "Prayer Station" in the atrium of City Hall operated by religious folks. The suit was successful, and the city was forced to allow the atheists to put up the Reason Station alongside the Prayer Station. My point in bringing up these examples is that all of these suggest that this group values reason.

The incredible irony here is that many of these groups and their websites trade primarily in invectives and vitriolic slams rather than any kind of reasoned defense. The dialogue surrounding the installment of the Reason Station, for example, was anything but thoughtful. You can go to their sites and see for yourself. If one dares to make a positive claim about God or Christianity (or any religion for that matter), one will find oneself mocked and ridiculed in real time, often with no critical reasoning in sight. Even with formal debates involving the so-called experts, it can be difficult to disentangle mocking complaints about religion from actual arguments on the atheist side.

I do not say this to match the ridicule. Rather, I mention this to point out a radical inconsistency in the current scene. This brand of atheism extols reason but tends not to engage thoughtfully and reasonably. Many have noted this inconsistency, even fellow atheists. Some professional philosophers who are avowed atheists have distanced themselves from the New Atheist movement. In fact, atheist philosopher Michael Ruse has said that Richard Dawkins's book *The God Delusion* has made him ashamed to be an atheist.[7] This is due to the fact that the philosophical arguments are weak, and there is no effort to deeply engage the views of the many very serious thinkers on the theistic side.

What's more is that the atheist will often act as if he or she never depends upon faith, only reason. This is ridiculous. The object of the atheist's faith

---

7   See Michael Ruse's Op Ed "Dawkins et al bring us into disrepute" by November 2, 2009 The Guardian.

may not be God or Scripture, but he or she will often have an undying faith in the ability of science to discover truths about (and beyond) the world. Theists will often point to features of the world that are inexplicable in an atheistic worldview, and the response is often faith of the fundamentalist sort that science will one day explain these facts. Moreover, the atheist will have faith in his or her senses, memory, the report of (select) books, and the powers of reason itself. The point is that the atheist exercises a more or less active trust in these things and is, therefore, equally a person of faith.

But there's a further irony here in the atheist's faith in reason. How faith-worthy is reason for the atheist? The atheist has a terrifically difficult time giving a reason *for reason*. To see this, we should note that reason is ultimately governed by principles of logic. What makes a claim reasonably supported is that the claim accords with the standards of logic. But the following also seems to be a legitimate question: What explains the system of logic itself? Here the atheist will be unable to cite anything that explains logic itself. The best the atheist can do is simply say that logic exists as a kind of brute, unexplained fact. But this starts to look like the atheist has an article of blind faith, which the atheist is so quick to decry.

By contrast, the theist has a perfectly good explanation for the values of logic. God himself, as the ultimate ground of all things, explains the theist's system of logic. God created matter and the physical laws of nature, but he is also the ground of all values, including logic, morality, and beauty. Logical principles are, in this view, the expression of the very mind of God.

It is always important to point out this is not to say that atheists cannot know the principles of logic and the standards of reasoning. But that's as far as it goes for the atheist. Their worldview does not seem to provide a ground for the principles of reason itself.

Now there is a lot more to be said on this issue. I haven't said, for example, how logical principles are grounded in the mind of God, and I do not have the space to do so here. But for our purposes, suffice it to say that Christian faith and reason are friendly concepts. God is the very ground of logic. So it seems that Christians should value the principles of logic and canons of reason precisely because, as Christians, we worship the God of logic.

3

God's Existence

The heavens pour forth their speech. –King David

In the first two chapters, I made the case that it is perfectly consistent with Christian faith to ask deep and difficult questions in search of good and reasonable answers for our faith. In fact, this should be a normal part of Christian discipleship as we seek to love God with our minds. We turn now to putting this into action. We'll explore some deep and difficult questions. This will not be an exhaustive treatment. It is intended to model how to begin exploring the big questions that relate to Christian faith. In this chapter, we'll think about reasons for believing God exists. In the next, we'll look at reasons for taking Christianity as true.

Arguments for God's existence are both powerful and plentiful, but sometimes, before you can say "Tylenol," they can jump to a high philosophical level. For example, philosophers don't know what to do with the existence of human consciousness (the basic awareness of our surroundings). Even if one thinks that one can thoroughly explain the human body in a naturalistic way, consciousness seems to inject into the picture something that goes beyond purely natural explanations (my thought that God loves me, for example, doesn't seem reducible to certain firings of the brain). In a purely natural world, the fact that we can reflect on and ask questions about life is very odd indeed. But in a Christian theistic picture, this problem of consciousness is not difficult to resolve since the Christian is not limited to natural entities in the first place. Theists have, therefore, argued that human consciousness seems to imply a theistic picture.

On another front, physicists continue to find ways in which the universe is balanced on a razor's edge. The values of the initial conditions of the universe had to be calibrated to such an infinitesimal degree for the universe to even exist, and especially for it to be a life-permitting universe, that it is exceedingly difficult to see this as a happy accident. It is really more like it rests on about 200 razors, all balanced on each other in a tall stack. Again, though the naturalist has a very difficult time explaining what appears to be a finely tuned universe, Christian theism has no such problem. Thus, theists have argued that the fine-tuning of the universe implies theism as well.

Both of these are powerful arguments for theism, and there is great value in studying and reflecting on them, but these arguments get technical in a hurry. We will attempt to avoid technicalities in making our case for God. I'm also convinced that there are many other reasons for believing in God that are quite compelling and can be grasped by our country grandma, children,[8] and anyone else who is able to reflect on what I think are obvious features of the world. This is not to say that the ensuing thoughts will be simple and easy. The point is that there are accessible reasons to believe in God. The versions of these reasons below aim to be accessible but may still be challenging in some ways if one is a novice. I think people generally have good reasons for believing in God. It's just that they haven't sufficiently thought these reasons through in order to articulate them. But they are there, and so let's love God with our minds as we reflect!

The reason for God

In Romans 1:20, Paul explicitly states that God has revealed various aspects about himself in the created world, and these aspects can be clearly seen. There's no shortage of opinions on how to understand this passage and what relevance it has for doing evangelism and apologetics. We certainly will not settle this debate in this short work, but it seems clear that this pas-

---

8 Some of the following discussion will be more accessible, and parts of it will be more difficult. My primary audience is not children, and so, though I'm convinced that small children can understand that the world points to a creator, this will not be explicitly framed in this way below. However, I will say that helping your children think of the world theistically is crucially important in raising kids with a robust Christian worldview.

sage indicates that we can know some things about God from the world, including that God exists.

Why do people believe God exists? I think the primary reasons are twofold. First, it is because the world only makes sense if there is a God. Second, it is because people have direct experiences of God.

Let's take these in turn.

The world makes sense if there is a God

There are a variety of facts that only make sense if God exists. Those facts are...

1. The existence of the universe itself
2. The exquisite design of the universe
3. Human value and purpose

These are all obvious facts of the world. One philosopher has defined the facts of common sense as those things that are "accepted by everyone (except some philosophers and some madmen)!"[9] This seems about right with the three facts listed above. But, at the same time, these are all curious facts. None of them had to be this way, and it makes sense to ask what explains why the world is this way. We see that these facts are well-explained (and many times only explained) by the hypothesis that there is a God.

Fact 1: The Universe itself

It is a curious fact that the universe exists at all. As children, we perhaps wondered why we, and all this other stuff, are here. It is very difficult to make sense of saying *it just had to be*. But here it is, and we want to ask why. Or more specifically, we want to ask what explanation is behind the fact that the universe exists.

Here's the basic idea. It certainly seems possible that the universe did not exist or that a very different universe existed. The universe is chock-full of what we'll call *contingencies*. It is typically thought that there are some

---

9   Huemer, Michael (2001) *Skepticism and the Veil of Perception* (Lanham, MD: Rowman & Littlefield), 18.

facts in the world that could not have been different. The truths of mathematics and logic, for example, are common examples of this sort. After all, how could the sum of 2 and 3 be anything other than 5? Contingencies, on the other hand, are ways the world is but didn't have to be. Consider, for example, the color of your car. It is a certain color (or combination of colors), but it could have been different. The physical universe could have been very different in many, many ways, and, even more importantly, it seems possible that the universe not exist at all. Because the universe seems to be itself contingent (i.e., could have failed to exist), it follows that there must be some cause for its existence that explains why it is the way it is. In short, the universe clearly seems to be an *effect*, and every effect requires a cause. In this discussion, we'll be guided by the following principle:

> *Contingency Principle: Every contingent thing requires a cause that explains that thing.*

This is such a plausible principle that it fuels most of science. In fact, it fuels almost every inquiry. When we see some sort of contingency, we immediately begin looking for the cause of the contingency. Suppose you come home to find your TV missing, and you notice that your window is also broken out. You may not know exactly what happened, but you would at least know that something (or more likely someone) is responsible for these contingent facts, and you wouldn't hesitate to call the police. A similar idea applies to the universe itself.

There are also striking scientific reasons for thinking that the universe came into existence a finite time ago, all charged up with energy, and has been winding down ever since. This beginning is commonly known as the *Big Bang*. Christians to whom I speak are sometimes very skeptical about the Big Bang. To be sure, there are likely beliefs within an overall Big Bang theory with which Christians may be uncomfortable, but the idea that there was a Big Bang that marked the beginning of the universe has theistic implications written all over it. That is, the fact that the universe had a sudden Big Bang seems to be something that requires a cause. To think that it just happened with no antecedent cause seems impossible.

You may be thinking, "Okay, the universe has a cause, but why think that this cause is God?" Well, it seems that the available options for possible causes of the universe itself become strikingly small. Perhaps there is some collection of contingent facts that gave rise to the universe. Perhaps, for example, there was a bigger bang that spawned a series of big bangs and multiple universes, including ours. This gives us a cause for our universe, but it is a contingent cause and, by the Contingency Principle, now the biggest bang is going to need a cause. This thesis looks like it merely pushes the question back one step without really explaining anything. You might hear scientists and philosophers making reference to such things as the multiverse or quantum fields as causes of the Big Bang. However, given the Contingency Principle, all of these are contingent facts that fall prey to needing some explanation.

We need something that is necessary (i.e., not contingent) that exists uncaused and can act without being acted upon. What can possibly fit this job description other than God? I know of no other necessary beings that can act without being acted upon. I'm not saying people can't dream up some alternative explanation, but the point is that the existence of a creator God, who is himself necessary, explains the contingent universe. It is a perfect fit, in fact, and thus provides us a compelling reason to believe in God.

Fact 2: The Design of the Universe

The existence of the universe is certainly a curious fact. However, there are many features *within* this universe that are also quite curious. We can sometimes stumble on good fortune. Sometimes a happy coincidence can feel like someone is "lookin' out for us," when, really, it was completely random and coincidental. However, when there is a highly improbable sequence of events, and these events seem fit together for a purpose, it is not unfair to begin to think that someone is, indeed, there! This is the way we find the universe. No one doubts that there are many extraordinary facts without which we couldn't exist. The debate is whether we simply lucked out or that these facts point to an intelligence that has designed the universe for a specific purpose—namely, our existence.

In fact, there are a number of famous atheists who have agreed that the design argument (especially when citing the features of its fine-tuning) the strongest argument there is for theism.[10] This is because there are a variety of features of our world that are make-your-head-explode unlikely. Here is what some eminent scientists have said:

> "A common sense interpretation of the facts suggests that a superintellect monkeyed with physics ... and that there are no blind forces worth speaking about in nature. The numbers one calculates from the facts seem to me so overwhelming as to put this conclusion almost beyond question." – Sir Fred Hoyle (astrophysicist and cosmologist, Cambridge University)[11]

> "There is for me powerful evidence that there is something going on behind it all ... it seems as though somebody has fine-tuned nature's numbers to make the universe. The impression of design is overwhelming." –P.C.W. Davies (physicist, Arizona State University)[12]

As I mentioned at the outset of the chapter, these details get technical in a hurry. To avoid the technical details, I want to suggest a thought experiment that effectively illustrates how a design argument is meant to work. Imagine waking up and finding yourself in an exquisitely designed biosphere on Mars where there is an incomprehensibly large amount of moving parts, and (catch this) all of them are necessary for you to survive in that environment.[13] One would have a lot of questions, the most pressing of which is how in the world you ended up on Mars! However, what you wouldn't ask is how this biosphere evolved by chance and natural forces. Instead, you would search high and low for those who were responsible for creating the biosphere with beings like you in mind. Even if you

---

10 In the film *Collision: Christopher Hitchens vs. Douglas Wilson*, Hitchens says at one point in a conversation with Wilson that the Fine-Tuning argument is the one argument that all atheists find intriguing. In an interview on the PBS show, *Closer to Truth*, Michael Shermer says the naturalistic explanation of the fine-tuning is not all that great and that this is the best argument on the side of theism.

11 Fred Hoyle, "The Universe: Past and Present Reflections." *Engineering and Science*, November, 1981. pp. 8–12

12 Paul Davies, *The Cosmic Blueprint: New Discoveries in Nature's Ability to Order the Universe* (West Conshohocken, PA: Templeton Foundation Press, 1989), p. 203

13 The example is borrowed from Robin Collins. See his "A Recent Fine-Tuning Design Argument" in *Christian Apologetics: An Anthology of Primary Sources*, edited by Swies, Khaldoun A. and Chad V. Meister (Grand Rapids, MI: Zondervan, 2012), 106.

couldn't find out who it was, you would rest assured that someone—some designer—at some point, was responsible for it.[14]

The reason this is a pertinent example is because the world really is just a biosphere. We have everything we need for a huge variety of biological life to thrive at the surface of our planet. But what could possibly explain why the earth would be chock-full of the incredible number of features necessary for life? Perhaps a handful of these can be explained naturalistically, but there is an overwhelming amount of features that do not seem to be explicable in naturalistic terms. Again, these facts lead us back to a designer.

Objection: God of the gaps?

It is often objected that all the theist is doing with a design argument is positing a God of the gaps. We don't know how to explain the earth as a biosphere (that is, there is a gap in our knowledge), and so the theist merely plugs in God. But the mere lack of explanation is not a good reason to assert that God exists.

In support of this objection, one typically brings up belief in the gods in ancient times. It is claimed that, early on in the history of intellectual thought, we did not understand much of the world. In this state of ignorance, it was common for people to posit the existence of gods in order to explain the unexplainable features of the world. Take a lightning storm, for example. In ancient times, we didn't understand extreme storms, and we especially didn't understand how bolts of lightning could flash across the sky. So, we posited some sort of divine activity that was responsible for hurling these bolts. The Greeks, for example, posited the existence of Zeus, and when there was a bad storm, they prayed to Zeus for mercy and attempted to appease him in some way or another. We now know via science how lightning works, and we no longer feel the need to think that we are possibly being aimed at when caught in a bad storm. With advancements in science, these gaps have gotten smaller and smaller, and so, though there are things we still do not understand, atheists argue that it is a mistake to posit the activity of a divine being.

---

14   For more on Intelligent Design, I would highly recommend "A Parent's Guide to Intelligent Design" at http://www.discovery.org/csc/back-to-school/

There are a few points with the god of the gaps objection that call for comment. The first is that, although discovering how lightning works rules out a limited god's role in a lightning storm, it does not rule out the existence of God. Using science, we can explain what happens in a weather system, and thus Zeus' role is eliminated. But no Christian thinks that God (emphasis on the capital "G" here) is hurling lightning bolts. In the Christian view, God created a world in which weather systems occur, and he holds each particular system together. God's role is not diminished in the slightest in our understanding of how this system works. Again, the fact that this sort of weather system exists points us squarely to a designer. John Lennox makes the point that understanding how an internal combustion engine works does nothing to rule out the contribution of Henry Ford in its development.[15] It seems silly to think that merely understanding how the engine works proves that there is no inherent design. In fact, it is exactly the opposite. Understanding how the engine works shows us that there is a need for a designer. And this holds true for the universe as well. The more we discover, the more we see evidence of design.

In summary, the design argument does not rest on what we do not know (i.e., the gaps). Rather, it is what we know about the world that points us to the existence of a designer.

Is the designer God? Again, the argument is that we need some explanation for why the world is so intricately designed for the existence of human life. The existence of an all-powerful, all-knowing God would perfectly explain why the universe is calibrated for human existence.

Fact 3: Human Value and Purpose

Almost everyone believes that other humans have value. It is not just that we ascribe value when someone is of value to us (e.g., our children, family members, or friends), but we think that, in general, it is wrong to intentionally kill or even harm another human being. This holds true for people who look very different from us and have different cultural habits from us. This also holds true even if the human lacks rational capacities (such as newborn babies and the mentally handicapped). We seem to think if one is human, then one has value no matter what. Even if one gets away with

---

15   See John Lennox (2009) *God's Undertaker: Has Science Buried God?* (Oxford: Lion Publishing), 47ff.

it scot-free, we typically think it is a gross and immoral violation to end the life of a human. But this is a curious fact. What does this fact indicate?

Does it indicate that we've socially evolved toward this end? This doesn't seem to explain this curious fact, since evolutionary explanations only work when there is some survival advantage. Is there a survival advantage for universally treating people with dignity and respect? History (and contemporary times) does not corroborate this notion. Societies have thrived with slave classes and with the devaluing of neighboring societies. Ancient Rome lasted an amazing 12 centuries despite the fact that they only extended universal rights to Roman citizens.

Moreover, an evolutionary explanation has a difficult time saying why one *ought* to follow a moral standard, especially when it is in our personal interest to break the standard and get away with it. The reason is that if evolution has programmed us to act morally, then it really isn't an objective right or wrong. What if I come to believe that evolution has merely programmed me to think some things are moral? What's stopping me from deciding to cast off my evolutionary urges and participate in morally reprehensible things when they are in my interest? What would the evolutionary theorist say? One could, I suppose, say that you should just continue to follow the urges. But why? Why *should* I follow evolutionary urges? It sounds like what's being said is that we are morally obligated to do so. But then moral obligation is something beyond the evolutionary urge. In this view, we are left without any reason why we should live our lives this way, unless, of course, it really is wrong to do morally reprehensible things.

The U.S. Declaration of Independence says:

> *We hold these truths to be self-evident, that all men are created equal, that they are endowed by their Creator with certain unalienable rights.*

Now consider the U.N. Declaration of Human Rights:

> *All human beings are born free and equal in dignity and rights. They are endowed with reason and conscience and should act towards one another in a spirit of brotherhood.*

Do you notice a significant difference in these two statements? They agree in declaring universal rights, but the U.N. Declaration leaves blank the exact explanation for why we are all equal in dignity and rights. What the U.S. Declaration includes is a *ground* for thinking all human beings are equal in certain unalienable rights. We have these rights precisely because God has endowed them to us.

It is important to note that we are not saying a nontheist cannot perfectly follow the U.N. Declaration and treat all human beings with respect and dignity. Indeed, sometimes nontheists do far better than Christians in treating each other with dignity. But treating people with equality and dignity is one thing; having a solid ground or explanation for doing so is an entirely different matter. The U.S. Declaration, by contrast, provides an explanation for the existence of rights and dignity.

Many people who reject the existence of a creator have a view very similar to the U.N. Declaration. They believe in moral standards and live overall moral lives. However, without a belief in God, there is nothing in their worldview that clearly supports this moral life. In many nontheistic views, humans are not categorically different from animals, insects, and bacteria. There seems to be nothing that allows me to systematically execute mosquitos but think at the same time that harming human beings is wrong.

We can deny that, at the end of the day, there really is a standard for how we live our lives, but we certainly all seem to live like we make a contribution to the world. Does it really matter whether we live our lives as saints or live them as the worst of sinners? Most of us think it does. But why should we unless there is this standard?

Again, the fact that we all value others and live as if we have significance is perfectly explained by the existence of God, who, so to speak, endows our lives with significance and value. In the Christian view, we are not merely molecules in motion, nor are we simply more advanced slime. We are embodied souls bearing the image of God, designed for the purpose of glorifying God. Our dignity and value, therefore, are not primarily found in our high level of neurological and biological functioning. There is something much deeper within our nature as humans. We can look different and act different from other humans, but this does not change our intrinsic natures. This deep intrinsic notion seems to track perfectly with the way in which we value human lives.

Who is this God?

Have we established the fact that God exists? Well, that depends on what we mean. None of these arguments by themselves *prove* that God exists. However, these few curious facts certainly seem to make the belief rational. This conclusion can and will be denied by those who want to deny it. But this is not written to convince atheists. Rather, it is written to help model how one might begin to investigate what reasons there are for concluding that God exists.

Does this give us the God of Abraham, Isaac, Jacob, and Jesus? Well, yes and no. The brief treatment above is all perfectly consistent with the biblical conception of God. In fact, I think that, in some ways, we have narrowed the conception quite strikingly. For one, if God is the first cause of the universe, then we must have a transcendent God powerful enough to create from nothing! This is not consistent with many non-Christian views of God. Moreover, God is responsible for astronomically precise calibration of the universe such that it is life-permitting rather than life-prohibiting. This would require God to be incredibly intelligent, if not omniscient. Furthermore, if God is the ground of morality, then he must be the very source of moral facts. This suggests that God must be essentially good. Even a God who could *possibly* do evil could not serve as the ground of moral goodness, because God's essentially good character is what fixes the moral standard for all moral agents.

With these arguments, we get a picture that does not necessarily fit in a wide variety of other traditions. But the picture is right at home in a Judeo-Christian tradition. Consider just a sampling of how Scripture pictures God:

> For by Him all things were created, both in the heavens and on earth, visible and invisible, whether thrones or dominions or rulers or authorities—all things have been created through Him and for Him. He is before all things, and in Him all things hold together. (Colossians 1:16-17)

> God, after He spoke long ago to the fathers in the prophets in many portions and in many ways, in these last days has spoken to us in His Son, whom He appointed heir of all

things, through whom also He made the world. (Hebrews 1:1-2)

"You alone are the Lord. You have made the heavens, the heaven of heavens with all their host, the earth and all that is on it, the seas and all that is in them. You give life to all of them and the heavenly host bows down before You. (Nehemiah 9:6)

These all speak to a conception of God who is responsible for creating and holding all aspects of our world together. For the Christian, God is the creator of the universe and has designed it with us in mind. As we see in the Colossians and Nehemiah passages, the world is all ultimately his, and it's all for him. This provides significance and purpose for every aspect of the Christian's life.

Experience of God

The second major reason people believe God exists is because, well, they run into him. From time to time, people have direct experiences of God himself. This is where one has experiences that are not plausibly explained in any way other than that God exists. It is actually very common for people to report having experiences that clearly seem to be supernatural. These include such things as miraculous events, healings, answers to prayer, and even an overwhelming sense of the presence of the divine.

Having a direct experience of something is the ideal reason for believing that the thing exists. You may have all the reason in the world to think something does not exist until that thing shows up and says, "Hi." However, direct experience of God is often criticized, not so much because folks don't have amazing stories that are impossible to explain away, but because these reports are overly common and point in too many different directions. Christians have stories, Mormons have stories, Muslims have stories, Hindus have stories, Spiritualists have stories, etc. and etc. Moreover, some Christians have a much greater emphasis on the supernatural, and it seems practically everything counts (in this view, getting to church on time with a prime parking spot is a miracle).

How do we sort out all of these reports? It seems to me that if God exists, we should expect there to be numerous reports of experiences of God, and having a genuine experience of God should serve as clear evidence that God exists for any particular person. With this said, I do agree with critics who say not every report (even of Christians) is accurate. People, for some reason, make up stories. Other times, people unintentionally make mistakes of interpretation. It could be that one has indeed had a supernatural experience but misattributed it to God. In the Christian view, the world is both natural and supernatural, and the supernatural realm includes far more beings than just God. Christians have always believed that there are angelic and demonic experiences, and I have little doubt that some experiences that people think are caused by God could be caused by demonic forces designed to confuse and distract people from truths about God.

Direct experiences can be the most powerful evidence one has, but, at the same time, experiences have at least two liabilities. First, it is easy to misinterpret experiences. We have to be very careful and judicious with what we take an experience to *mean*. What happens is one thing; what it all means is another. So, I think we can reasonably infer that God exists on the basis of clear experiences that are only explicable on the thesis that God is real. However, it is often precarious to begin to fill in specific doctrine on the basis of experience alone.

Secondly, experiences of God are often very individualistic as they relate to evidence for the existence of God. Experiences such as these are not repeatable or sharable affairs as experiences. The arguments discussed above are ones that anyone can use as evidence for the existence of God once they are understood, and they can be recounted to anyone. However, when we hear a story about a person who has had some unusual experience, although such a story can bless us and build our faith, when the experience hasn't happened to us, we need to be very careful how such a report informs our views.

Conclusion

When it comes to reasons for thinking God exists, to say that we've only touched the tip of the iceberg would be an understatement. I've only attempted to indicate lines of thinking that point to the existence of God in accessible ways. There is so much more!

I've argued first that there are a variety of facts that make best sense if God exists. The three facts that I mentioned were the existence of the universe itself, the intricate design of the universe, and the value and moral significance of each and every human being. By contrast, the obvious features of life make little sense if God doesn't exist.

Secondly, I argued that people have experiences of God. This is not all that uncommon. Although there are certain liabilities with the evidential value of experiences, when we come into the presence of God, there is a lot that changes for us, including our knowledge of him who is there.

Christianity

Lord, to whom shall we go? You [Jesus] have the words of eternal life. We have come to believe and to know that you are the Holy One of God. –Simon Peter

We turn now to consider reasons for thinking Christianity is true. We should remind ourselves that we are not looking to give an exhaustive proof of Christianity. Rather, we love God with our minds by exploring the evidence for Christianity specifically. There are many different narratives out there for how to understand God, and so we should have some reasons for thinking that Christianity has it right. For many, Christianity is thought of as merely one among many religious traditions. I will begin by arguing that Jesus, his teaching, and the movement he started stand out from all the rest. This is not necessarily to say that the tradition is thereby true, but for the reasons I detail below, Christianity has a richness that should make it intriguing to all.

Jesus as a standout[16]

The first reason Jesus is a standout is because the Christian narrative has always attempted to provide *evidence* for its core claims. This is really quite extraordinary when one thinks about it. The central claims about Jesus

16 Some of this material was adapted from a presentation given by Craig Hazen at Biola University in the fall of 2003 for why a seeker should start with Christianity. Hazen has developed this material into a book called *Five Sacred Crossings: A Novel Approach to a Reasonable Faith* (Eugene, OR: Harvest House Publishers, 2008).

crucially involve historical claims. In fact, in 1 Corinthians 15:12-19, Paul says that the very truth of Christianity decisively turns on the historicity of the resurrection. That is, this is not something that happened in an inaccessible spiritual realm. Rather, this is about a real event in history, publically witnessed by real people, both friends and foes. Thus the claims about Jesus are based on the reliable witness of those who were very close to these situations, many of whom were actual eyewitnesses. We should underscore how unusual this is in religious literature. You don't see an emphasis on evidence and eyewitnesses in any other tradition that I'm aware of. The upshot of this for seekers is that, internal to the view, it is a way to verify if it is true or falsify if it is false. Other religious traditions perhaps have some way to verify (e.g., the Mormon looks for a burning in the bosom), but they would be hard-pressed to say what would actually falsify the view were it to be false. Not so with the Christian tradition.

A second reason Christianity stands out is that Jesus is involved in virtually every other religious tradition. Everyone wants a piece of Jesus! In Islam, he is a central prophet. In Buddhism, he is a bodhisattva, or enlightened one. Even in Judaism, it is not uncommon to think that he was an important rabbi. He is, of course, central to all non-orthodox Christian sects, such as Mormonism, Jehovah's Witnesses, and Christian Science. Also, it is very common for contemporary non-Christian religious movements to make a place for Jesus, including Scientology and Baha'i. Even atheists will say that he was a good moral teacher! There is no other religious figure that has this kind of centrality across traditions. Christianity is the only one that keeps this figure that everyone wants, Jesus, at its very center.

A third reason is that Christianity purports to actually solve the human predicament and cause human flourishing (more on this below). I'm not interested in a new set of rules and rituals. I'm not interested in merely adopting a new culture. I want to be made right, to be made whole. Any religion that does not promise this is, in my view, not worth our time. Christianity's promise is bigger than any religion I know of. It does not merely provide a new set of rules, and if I'm successful in following those rules, then I find my way into paradise. It provides a way to be made new. It's that good and that intriguing!

The fourth reason Jesus is a standout is that the Christian narrative nicely fits with the conception of God that results from the many arguments for God's existence (some of which were highlighted in chapter 3). This is not a knock-down-drag-out argument, but there would definitely be some tension in asserting a theistic narrative that doesn't square with the arguments for God's existence. For example, if we have successfully argued that moral facts imply the existence of God, who is the ground of morality, then it is problematic, to say the least, if a religious tradition does not picture God as the ground of morality (such as some versions of Islam). Also, since there is reason to think that God created the universe, this becomes a difficulty for a tradition that thinks God is part of the universe (such as Mormonism). However, Christianity fits with all of the prominent arguments for God's existence.

Again, none of these reasons makes it such that Christianity is thereby true. And I have merely pointed at these facts without really arguing for them. However, these four facts help us see the richness of Christianity and hopefully leave one wanting to explore further.

What reason do we have for believing in Christianity?

In a famous passage in C.S. Lewis' *Mere Christianity*, Lewis points out how preposterous it is to claim that Jesus is merely a good moral teacher. Though Jesus is, of course, a good moral teacher, Lewis reminds us that Jesus made many claims that go beyond moral teaching. Lewis says, "He claims to forgive sins. He says He has always existed. He says He is coming to judge the world at the end of time."[17] What makes this especially amazing is the Jewish context within which Jesus speaks. The Jews were clear that these were actions only performed by God, and for the Jew, no sane person would ever make himself out to be God. "And when you have grasped that," Lewis says, "you will see that what this man said was, quite simply, the most shocking thing that has ever been uttered by human lips."[18]

Lewis goes on to say:

> A man who was merely a man and said the sort of things
> Jesus said would not be a great moral teacher. He would

---

17   C.S. Lewis (1952) *Mere Christianity* (New York, NY: Harper Collins Publishers), 51.

18   Ibid.

either be a lunatic—on a level with the man who says he is
a poached egg—or else he would be the Devil of Hell. You
must make your choice. Either this man was, and is, the
Son of God: or else a madman or something worse. You
can shut Him up for a fool, you can spit at Him and kill
Him as a demon; or you can fall at His feet and call Him
Lord and God. But let us not come with any patronizing
nonsense about His being a great human teacher. He has
not left that open to us. He did not intend to.[19]

According to Lewis, Jesus cannot merely be a good moral teacher and say
the things he said. He would either have been lying about these things or
perhaps poached-egg-level crazy. But if either of these were true, he would
not be a good moral teacher. If we are to say that he is a good moral teacher,
then our only option is to call him Lord.

I think this is a compelling argument, but there is a problem. This trilemma does not exhaust all of the available options. What if, for example,
he really didn't claim to forgive sins? Here is a possibility: he could have
been a good moral teacher whose followers later embellished what he said
and did. Thus, it's not that he is liar, lunatic, or Lord, because it is also possible that Jesus (or at least the extraordinary material about him) is merely
legend. So, on this response, though there could be bits of truth in the Gospel accounts, it is generally thought that the truth is mired in legendary
development, and this hopelessly skews what we are to believe about him.

Is the Bible Historically Reliable?

The charge that the Bible is filled with legendary development calls into
question the reliability of Scripture. We'll constrain our discussion to the
reliability of our accounts about Jesus found in Scripture.

The idea that the stories of Jesus are mostly legendary is practically standard in the broader community of critical New Testament scholars. Many
of them think, when it comes to studying the life of Jesus, there was likely
a real person of history who garnered a following of Jewish believers but
was then killed by the Romans. The claim is that his followers were so

---

19 Ibid., 52

moved by him and simultaneously so devastated at his death that they began honoring him by telling stories about him. The stories started out small and mostly accurate. But then, just like the old telephone game, as the stories got passed around, they changed. In fact, they got "better" and more embellished. As time went by, the stories got huge, and before we knew it, we had folks claiming a dying and rising Son of God. Scholars attempt to somehow carve out from the Gospel accounts what's known as the "historical Jesus," who is supposed to be a gifted teacher or perhaps a political zealot. The historical Jesus is taken to be different from the legendary and mythical figure they call the "Christ of Faith," who developed in the minds of his followers and found his way into the New Testament sometime after his crucifixion.

Legends

Let's take a closer look at legends. Legends take time. Let's say I go fishing with some friends out in the deep sea and catch a fish. Let's say it is a scrawny little six-incher unworthy of the bait it just consumed. But I show my fishing buddies my prize. Imagine later that day I claim to have caught a 6-foot marlin. This is never going to fly (or swim!) with my buddies, since, as eyewitnesses, they would instantly disconfirm my claim.

However, suppose I keep quiet about my fish. I let a few years go by. I begin talking about my six-incher, and a year later the six-incher becomes a seven-incher. If the fish in my story slowly gets bigger and bigger, could it then become a six-foot marlin? It's not clear that it can. Some legendary development of my story can happen (a few inches may be tolerated) but it cannot turn into something radically different (such as a six-foot prize fish) if the eyewitnesses are still in the picture. If the eyewitnesses are around, then I will still not get away with my myth, even if significant time has passed.

Now we obviously forget details of events, especially when we don't really care about the event or the specific details of the event. But notice that, even if my buddies couldn't remember the exact size of my fish, they likely could remember whether I pulled out a marlin, the queen of the sport fish. Most people do not get to see a marlin reeled in, and fishing enthusiasts would likely remember whether this happened or didn't happen even decades later. In order for my marlin story to be successful, my fishing buddies must no longer be in the picture. This either takes a significant passage of time or relocation, or perhaps both.

Jesus' ministry was public. This means that there were many eyewitnesses to what happened around the time of Jesus' crucifixion. Also, the location of the birth of the Christian church is without dispute. There's little doubt that it began in precisely the same region where Jesus was crucified. So as long as these accounts date early enough, there would have been many eyewitnesses who could either confirm or disconfirm what happened during the time of Jesus. The real question becomes whether or not there is enough time for legendary development.

It is estimated that legends, especially when they are about significant events, take at least three generations to develop.[20] We are talking about at least 100 years, and I should emphasize the "at least" here. This is the bare minimum. With some historical figures, it is more like 500 years before we begin to see clear embellishments of historical accounts. But to be on the safe side, let's say that if an account about Jesus dates within the first century (roughly within 70 years of the events they record), then it is implausible to think it contains significant legendary development.

Close

Let's zoom out to the turn of the first century (A.D. 100). What do we know is going on? At around this time, there is a Roman historian by the name of Tacitus writing about the history of Rome from the time of the Emperors Tiberius (A.D. 14) to Nero (A.D. 68). The ministry of Christ falls squarely within this time period, including the time of his death at around A.D. 33. In discussing Nero, Tacitus writes of Nero's falsely accusing Christians for the great fire of Rome and his ruthless persecution of them for this reason. According to Tacitus:

> ...to suppress the rumor, [Nero] falsely charged with the guilt, and punished with the most exquisite tortures, the persons commonly called Christians, who were hated for their enormities. Christus, the founder of the name,

---

20   See William Lane Craig *The Son Rises* (Chicago, IL: Moody Press, 1981), 101 for a discussion of the development of legend.

was put to death by Pontius Pilate, procurator of Judea in the reign of Tiberius: but the pernicious superstition, repressed for a time, broke out again, not only through Judea, where the mischief originated, but through the city of Rome also. (*Annals* 15:44)

We see two things with the Tacitus passage. We see some of the facts surrounding the life of Christ corroborated just as they are recorded in the New Testament. We have his death by crucifixion by Pontius Pilate and the time—namely, during the reign of Tiberius. We also see that he is not a fan of Christianity. He calls it a "pernicious superstition" that has broken out throughout Judea and the city of Rome. This implies that it has broken out across a huge swath of area. It is no minor Jewish cult by the time Nero is in power (less than 35 years!), but Christianity is a force in its own right in the Empire.

What is this "pernicious superstition" that has made its way all the way to the consciousness of a Roman Emperor to the degree that it has earned his ire? Could we plausibly believe that it is Jesus' moral teaching? I don't know about you, but to me, the teachings "Blessed are the peacemakers for they will be called children of God" and "If anyone slaps you on the right cheek, turn to them the other cheek also" aren't "enormities" worthy of "exquisite tortures." For a Roman Emperor to be bothered with this, we need something far more extraordinary.

We know what the New Testament identifies as the extraordinary event: the resurrection of Jesus Christ. But the resurrection is supposed to be the primary legend that Jesus' followers created. However, this is a difficulty, because we are only 35 years away from the time of Christ. It would be difficult for this legend to be propagated at this early date.

Closer

We must admit that a lot can happen in 35 years, so let's zoom in a bit further. We'll begin at the book of Acts. The book of Acts reads as a rather factual narrative and purports to provide the history of the early church from its inception. What we notice about Acts is that it ends with Paul awaiting trial in Rome. This is strange, since we know there were catastrophic events that occurred just after this time. The book of Acts leaves out the persecution of Christians by Nero, which likely involved the execution of Paul (A.D. mid-60s), and the destruction of the Temple (A.D. 70). Since the book of Acts chronicles these sorts of events (especially the life of Paul), there is only one plausible explanation for its silence on these matters: Acts was written before these events occurred. This plausibly dates the book of Acts to the early 60s. The author of the book of Acts is Luke. Luke is also the author of the Gospel of Luke. It is widely believed that the Gospel of Luke is written before the book of Acts. This plausibly puts the Gospel of Luke in the mid- to late 50s, just over 20 years after the events it describes.

Now 20 years sounds to our modern ears like an extraordinary amount of time. We are used to hearing reports practically in real time about events that may be happening on the other side of the globe! But when it comes to ancient accounts, 20 years is extraordinarily good, at least as it relates to the broad details of an account. Remember, a legend requires at least three generations to develop. Perhaps some of the fringe details could have been changed, but the broad and major details could not be plausibly changed given that there would be too many eyewitnesses who could confirm or disconfirm these claims.

Let's think a bit more about the passage of 20 years and whether one would be able to recount what happened 20 years prior. If you are sufficiently old enough (you probably have to be 30 or older for this to work), try to remember where you were 20 years ago. For me, I was in college. If you asked me *precisely* what I was doing exactly 20 years ago, I really would be at a loss to say with any kind of accuracy. But I remember the town I was living in and broadly what I was doing at that time. However, if you said, "Hey, remember that time the men's dorm burnt to the ground?" I would, with great confidence, say that this, in fact, never happened. I am 100 percent confident that the men's dorm did not burn down during my time at college. Why? *Because that's the sort of detail I would remember if it had actually happened.* If the men's dorm had burnt to the ground, I would likely remember the main contours of the event. If an event is significant enough, you often hear people say, "I remember like it was yesterday," and they can recount details with amazing accuracy. So 20 years is really quite good for ancient sources.

Really, really close

The case gets better still. We can zoom in even further. Many people do not realize this, but the letters of Paul are the earliest documents of the New Testament, and many of them are regarded by critical scholars as authentic (esp. 1 and 2 Corinthians, Galatians, and Romans). These are typically dated to the early to mid-50s, which places them at or within 20 years of Jesus' ministry. Paul saw his ministry as one of pointing to Christ, and he does so with deep theological themes. Here is some of what Paul mentions related to the life of Christ:

1. His virgin birth (Gal. 4:4)

2. His titles of Deity (Rom. 1:3-4; 10:9)

3. His sinless life (1 Cor. 5:21)

4. His death on the cross (Rom. 4:25; 5:8; Gal. 3:13)

5. That he died to pay for our sins (1 Cor. 15:3; 2 Cor. 5:21; cf. Mark 10:45)

6. His burial (1 Cor. 15:4)

7. His resurrection on the "third day" (1 Cor. 15:4)

8. His post-resurrection appearances to the apostles and others (1 Cor. 15:5-8)[21]

What we see here is that, well within the lifetime of many of those who would have witnessed these events, a very high Christology already exists. That is to say, within two decades, we have Paul identifying these core facts about Jesus, all of which make it impossible to think that these themes developed late as a legendary tradition.

Now, the likely response to this is that we still have a considerable amount of time between the events and the accounts. It would be nice if we could get closer than this. And indeed we can. We cannot get every detail, but we can get the Gospel.

A 20-year gap is quite extraordinary. What follows simply boggles the mind!

---

21 This is taken from Norman Geisler (2013) *Christian Apologetics* (Grand Rapids, MI: Baker Academic), 351. He includes a list of 27 distinct facts that we can take from these four letters about the understanding of Christ.

New Testament scholars are able to discern when a portion of the text is an early creed. A creed is a formulation of key doctrine set in a memorable and summarized fashion. The thing about a creed is that it dates earlier than the text in which it is embedded, since the creed is typically already in use. There's one such creed in 1 Corinthians 15. Recall that 1 Corinthians is considered authentic by a majority of critical scholars. So, 1 Corinthians is already on good historical ground. Paul begins 1 Corinthians 15 by saying he wants to remind the Corinthian believers of the Gospel. He then says:

> For I delivered to you as of first importance what I also received, that Christ died for our sins *according to the Scriptures*, and that He was buried, and that He was raised on the third day *according to the Scriptures*, and that He appeared to Cephas, then to the twelve. After that He appeared to more than five hundred brethren at one time, most of whom remain until now, but some have fallen asleep; then He appeared to James, then to all the apostles; and last of all, as to one untimely born, He appeared to me also. (emphasis added)

We should notice that Paul begins by indicating that what he is about to say is something he received and is now passing on to them. Notice my italicized phrases that repeat "according to the Scriptures," which occur in verses 3 and 4. This is meant to give the passage a certain rhythm, and these facts together suggest this is an early creed.

In terms of the content of the creed, there are a number of important points. It mentions the death of Jesus. But notice his death was for a purpose, namely, "for our sins." We see a theological understanding of his death already present in this early creed. There is also a clear affirmation of Jesus' resurrection, and Paul proceeds to ground these truths in eyewitness testimony.

The big question is when did Paul receive this creed? That is, when should we date this creed? Well, let's ask a scholar. John Dominic Crossan has said:

> Paul wrote to the Corinthians from Ephesus in the early 50s C.E. But he says in 1 Corinthians 15:3 that 'I handed

on to you as of first importance which I in turn received.' The most likely source and time for his reception of that tradition would have been Jerusalem in the early 30s when, according to Galatians 1:18, he 'went up to Jerusalem to visit Cephas [Peter] and stayed with him fifteen days.'[22]

Did you catch that? This places the dating of this creed, according to Crossan, in the "early 30s," when Paul would have had contact with the other apostles. Jesus died when? In the early 30s! This dates to just after (if not concurrent with) the events it describes, replete with the theological understanding of Jesus' death and resurrection grounded in eyewitness testimony!

It is worth pointing out who John Dominic Crossan is. Crossan is one of the cofounders and most prominent members of the Jesus Seminar, which was a group of liberal scholars who were extremely critical of the biblical accounts of Jesus. Each member of the Jesus Seminar would vote on which sayings of Jesus should be considered authentic. The group only had confidence in about 20 percent of the sayings of Jesus. Crossan is no friend of the Gospel, and yet even he thinks this creed dates almost concurrent with the events it recounts.

And this is not unique to Crossan. According to New Testament scholar Gary Habermas, "most of the critical scholars who date these events conclude that Paul received this material within just a few years after Jesus' death, in the early or mid-30s."[23] Habermas goes on to cite dozens of critical scholars who agree. We are looking at this material dating no more than 2-7 years after the events and as early as a matter of months! This is truly exceptional!

The single most important event in the entire Bible for the Christian tradition has historical evidence that dates within a handful of years and perhaps months of the event. There is simply no way in which the resurrection is a legendary development. It arises from the very beginning and is the very same message on which the Christian Gospel turns.

---

22   John Dominic Crossan (2001) *Excavating Jesus: Beneath the Stones, Behind the Texts* (New York, NY: Harper Collins), 254.

23   Gary Habermas "The Case for the Resurrection" in To *Everyone An Answer: A Case for the Christian Worldview* (Downers Grove, IL: InterVarsity Press, 2004), 184.

In summary, what we see is explosive growth that spreads across the Roman Empire (and eventually takes over the Empire) in a relatively short amount of time. The message that caught fire is that Jesus Christ did not stay dead but defeated death and sin in the resurrection. This message dates to the very beginning and is grounded in eyewitness testimony. Could they be lying about it? Though it is possible, it is extremely difficult to see how they could do this and, more importantly, why they would do this. Most of these eyewitnesses were persecuted horribly and ultimately martyred precisely because of this message. The most plausible explanation for this is that they witnessed to something extraordinary. At a certain point, I think we need to simply take these witnesses at their word and believe that the event that changed their lives was bearing witness to the risen Christ.

If we've successfully ruled out the possibility of legend, then Lewis' trilemma can be reestablished. If Jesus is to be taken seriously, it seems our only option is to call him Lord!

The Brilliance of the Gospel

As the foregoing makes clear, there is good historical evidence for the truth of Christianity. However, I think there is another powerful way to argue for this that points to the beauty and brilliance of the Gospel. My thesis is that Christianity is not merely rational to believe on intellectual grounds, but that it is incredibly attractive, as well. In short, the Gospel is brilliant. It is both intellectually smart and, at times, blindingly beautiful.

First, what is the Gospel? Here is a brief summary:

God creates the world, not arising from a need but out of love and for his glory. The Gospel is decidedly not about us, and it is not about what we can get out of it. Instead, **God is the end of our salvation**. It is about bringing glory to him.

However, humans freely sin. **Our sin is the need for salvation**. Given the fact that we have chosen to go against the moral law written on all of our hearts, we are under the condemnation of God as the holy and righteous Judge.

But, and here is the good news, Jesus Christ pays the penalty in our place on the cross and defeats sin by rising again. **Jesus Christ is the basis of**

our salvation. God, in his grace and mercy, has provided a way of salvation, and this is precisely in the person and work of Jesus Christ. God's justice is perfectly satisfied, and his love and mercy for us is expressed. Jesus is the solution to our sin problem.

Given this work, we are called to place our faith in Christ. **Faith is the means of our salvation**. It is important to mention that this does not earn our salvation, since salvation has already been earned. It is simply coming to see that God is God—the ultimate end—and repenting of the ways in which we have self-served. This, of course, means that, given our salvation, we seek to live in such a way that everything we do is for him!

The result of salvation: we are rightly restored and properly oriented to bring glory to God.

Before we move on, I must confess that even though I have been thinking about these truths for decades, I still find myself in awe. I'm a philosopher trained at a high level of analytic philosophy. I have read many of the greatest minds who have ever lived, and in my opinion, there's nothing quite like the Gospel. I still find myself hearing this afresh and am forced to pause in wonder at the beauty and brilliance of the Gospel. I find it simply the most amazing and breathtaking series of thoughts ever offered.

But there's more. Let's speak a bit more about the Gospel's brilliance.

The Gospel is decidedly unexpected. That is, if this were man-made, we'd expect it to be aimed at us. But this is not a humanistic Gospel. We benefit massively, to be sure, but this is only through surrendering our lives to Christ as Lord. Unfortunately, there are people who present the Gospel as a kind of sales pitch, but the Gospel is not about us or securing our spot within eternal bliss. Our eternity is more of a byproduct of our making Christ the Lord of our lives. G.K. Chesterton once said, "Truth, of course, must of necessity be stranger than fiction, for we have made fiction to suit ourselves."[24] There is a way in which the Gospel does not at all suit our fancies, since it points us away from ourselves.

However, the Gospel is exactly what we need. The Gospel perfectly fits our need and satisfies the human predicament. I find that most people

---

24   Chesterton, GK *Heretics* (CreateSpace Independent Publishing Platform, 2009), 23.

will admit that, though we may be capable of good, we all fall far short of perfection. We may want to do good, we may even try to do good, but we often do not achieve the good. Almost every worldview offers some sort of solution to this human predicament. I don't have the space to canvass the different proposals, but in effect, what they all have in common is they give us something to do. But how can *doing something* possibly constitute a solution to the human predicament? We should keep in mind that our problem in the first place is that we have a moral problem. We don't *do* what we are supposed to do in the first place. How does giving us a new list of things to do even sort of solve the problem?

Let me illustrate this with an example. Suppose you have a nasty fall and break your leg. Let's say you go to the doctor, and he tells you that you indeed have a fracture. The doctor says, "My prescribed treatment for your condition is to get up and *walk it off*." Wait, what? Precisely how is walking off a broken leg supposed to help the broken leg? The problem, as it currently stands, is that you can't walk, so trying to walk will only exacerbate the problem. It would be at this point that I'd suggest getting a new doctor.

In the same way, no amount of attempting to live a good life, the life of a religious tradition, or even the life of a "good Christian," for that matter, will help our human predicament, because our problem is precisely that we cannot live the way we are supposed to live in the first place. If your religion or denomination is merely telling you to do things to help your condition, then I'd suggest you get yourself a new religion or denomination.

To be clear, I'm not saying that religious performances are unimportant. But, in the Christian view, doing things should be an expression of our faith, not a prerequisite for faith. Indeed, James says that our faith is dead without deeds (James 2:17). But if salvation is predicated on living a certain moral lifestyle, then this thing is hopeless. Let me just be honest: if it is up to me to perform, then I'm doomed.

There is perhaps no more profound truth on which to reflect related to this topic than Paul's statement, "For by grace you have been saved through faith" (Eph. 2:8a). Just let that sink in for a moment. Our salvation is by grace. It is not by works. It is completely giving up that secures our salvation. It is the work of the perfect man, God in the flesh, that has earned our salvation. This is amazing and wondrous in its implications!

You should know that this is *completely unique* to Christianity. There's not a religion in the history of the world that predicated salvation on grace by faith. Though this points us away from ourselves, it is precisely what makes us whole and makes us flourish. There's a certain beauty and brilliance to these profound truths that are so very attractive and ultimately point us to the divine.

5

Objections

Quite often, we naturally gravitate to social groups that share our funda-
mental convictions. This is true politically, socially, and especially theologically. We tend to cluster with those who believe and value things that are
very similar to what we believe and value. The downside to this homoge-
neity is that it is often difficult to see the weaknesses in our own views. It is
often only when someone challenges us from the outside, so to speak, that
we begin to notice our blind spots, and it can be quite stressful when we
suddenly realize we've believed something uncritically.

It seems to me that committing to the apologetic approach I outlined in
the first two chapters can prevent many of these shocks to our system. It
should be very natural for us to be asking deep and difficult questions of
our faith in safe contexts as part of our love and pursuit of God.

So far, we have looked at positive reasons for the core truths of Christianity. We now turn to asking some critical questions that have, for some,
acted as objections to Christianity. I'd first like to highlight a few objections that are very popular but are not as difficult. We will then turn to a
couple of objections that are much more serious challenges.

The Injustices of the Church?

A very common means for objecting to Christianity is pointing to the heinous and evil acts that have been perpetuated in the name of Christ throughout the history of the Christian church. The usual suspects for this type of charge include the Crusades, the various inquisitions, slavery in the U.S. and elsewhere, and, in more recent times, the alleged cover-ups of child molestation cases in the effort to protect offending clergymen.

Our initial reaction might be: so what? Just because someone has done something evil does not make the view they happen to hold thereby false or problematic. It's clear that people have done terrible things in the name of Christ and apparently for Christ's sake. That is, there's no question that we have some black marks in our history. However, show me a view that has no black marks, and I'll show you a view that has no human adherents. It seems to be the case that if there are morally imperfect humans in the mix, then you will have morally imperfect actions from time to time.

The objection can't be merely that there have been some people who just happen to be Christians who have done terrible things. For unjust actions to be a problem for a view, the actions must be specifically commanded or endorsed by that view. If a view commanded or endorsed child abuse, for example, then this would indeed be a problem for that view, given the immorality of child abuse.

If this is right, then we have to ask whether the injustices in the history of the Christian church are commanded or even just endorsed by the Christian view.

I want to suggest a helpful way to go about answering this question. The strategy I suggest is to decide on what we'll call an exemplar. An exemplar is a person who, on all accounts, best lives out the teachings of the view. Next, we look to see whether the unjust actions in question are consistent with the life and teachings of the exemplar. If they are, then the injustice is a problem. If they are not, then the problem is resolved.

Who is the exemplar when it comes to Christianity? Well, of course, this would be Jesus Christ.

Now let's look at some moral wrong that was committed by the Christian Church. Let's look at something like conversion by the sword, which occurred during the Spanish Inquisition in the 15th century. Here, Jews and Muslims were under threat of death and violent torture if they did not convert to Christianity and "freely" undergo baptism into the Roman Catholic Church (it is "free" because one could choose death instead). Is conversion by the sword consistent with the life and teachings of Jesus Christ? It is exceedingly difficult to see how this could be so. There is not an instance of coercion in the entire record of Jesus' life. He proselytized, but only in a way that attracted people to follow him. It is exceedingly difficult to see how one reconciles these evangelistic practices of Jesus with the conversion by the sword of the inquisitions.

It seems, therefore, that the inquisitions are clearly out of step with the life and teaching of Jesus and, by extension, are not a problem of the view itself. We can agree that these were moral wrongs, and we should condemn these wrongs for the evil that they are, but they don't seem to present any specific problem for the Christian view since the Christian view does not endorse forced conversion.

Though I will not explore the issue here, it is instructive to come up with the exemplar of other traditions, as well, and ask whether the injustices committed by adherents to those religions are out of step with their exemplars.

(Alleged) Contradictions of Scripture?

It is very common for someone to object to Christianity based on the belief that there is a wide array of contradictions in the Bible. It is also very common that, if pressed, the person raising this objection cannot name a single contradiction. However, it doesn't take but an Internet search of "Bible contradictions" to provide an abundance of opportunities to think about possible inconsistencies. The reality is that there are a number of passages that appear to be in conflict.

Let's get clear on what a contradiction is. A contradiction is when a claim (e.g., x is good) and the negation of the claim (e.g., x is not good) are both asserted as true, where the terms of the claims are understood in the very same sense and occurring at the same time. Those latter qualifications are important. Suppose you heard me say, "Pizza is good." Suppose, a few minutes later, you heard me say, "Pizza is not good." Have I, thereby, contradicted myself? Not necessarily. We can mean a lot of different things by the word "good." It could be that we mean good *in taste*, or we could mean good *in nutrition*, or perhaps there are other meanings as well. If I meant two different things, then I haven't contradicted myself. Furthermore, I could be referring to different times in my life where I enjoyed pizza and other times in which I didn't, and these would, again, not be contradictory. But if two inconsistent statements have terms that mean the same thing and refer to the same time, then the statements are contradictory.

It is important to mention that when it comes to the Bible, the reason there are so many apparent inconsistencies is because the Bible is a multi-authored, multi-genre book with many different aims and purposes relative to specific sections of Scripture written over the better part of two millennia! Many of the apparent inconsistencies can be resolved by simply thinking about the genre, the purpose of the relevant texts, and what was going on historically at the time the text was written.

Let's look at a few examples of alleged contradictions.

Should I honor my father and mother or not?

Exodus 20:12 records the command "Honor your father and your mother," while Jesus says in Luke 14:26, "If anyone comes to Me, and does not hate his own father and mother and wife and children and brothers and sisters, yes, and even his own life, he cannot be My disciple." On a straightforward reading, this would appear to be a contradiction about how one should think about one's parents. However, this is easily reconciled once we realize that Jesus is using hyperbolic language to communicate how "sold-out" a disciple must be. After all, Jesus is in the midst of speaking in parables and teaching in the most extreme terms about the devotion of a disciple. Jesus doesn't think that we should hate our family members any more than he thinks we should carry literal lumber on our backs to fulfill his command to carry our cross (v. 27). The point is to stress that the Christian commitment is all-pervasive. Once we understand the genre of the Luke passage, we see that this is not difficult to reconcile with the Exodus passage.

Just who came to the empty tomb?

Perhaps the most often cited examples of contradiction are the events related to the resurrection of Christ as recounted in the four Gospels. One instance concerns the women to whom Jesus appeared after the resurrection. We, in fact, find four different lists of women in each of the four Gospels:

Matthew: "Mary Magdalene and the other Mary" (Matt. 28:1)

Mark: "Mary Magdalene, and Mary the mother of James, and Salome" (Mark 16:1)

Luke: "Mary Magdalene and Joanna and Mary the mother of James; also the other women with them" (Luke 24:10)

John: "Mary Magdalene" (John 20:1)

What we see common to all of these is, of course, the mention of Mary Magdalene. Now, if the John passage said that Mary Magdalene came by herself, or if the Luke passage said that Mary Magdalene was not present, then it would be impossible to reconcile these passages with the other Gospel accounts. But as it is, to claim that Mary Magdalene came to the tomb is perfectly consistent with saying that Mary Magdalene *and* other women came to the tomb.

To better understand this, suppose I have two students, Bob and Joe, who come to my office to discuss philosophy. If I were to run into Bob's parents later on, I might report to them only that Bob came to my office. Perhaps they don't know Joe, and so it would be pointless to mention the fact that Joe also came to the office. However, if, after this, my dean asked me whether any students came to office hours, I would tell him that Bob and Joe both came. I haven't contradicted myself, because saying Bob and Joe came to my office is perfectly consistent with saying Bob came to my office. Again, it would only be a contradiction if I said that Bob came to my office *by himself*.

Or, for another example that likely captures what's going on in the biblical accounts above, suppose the president of Southwestern Seminary, Paige Patterson, stopped by my office along with his administrative team, Bob and Joe. Notice I can describe this situation in a perfectly consistent manner by saying, "Dr. Patterson stopped by my office," or, "Dr. Patterson and some others stopped by my office," or "Dr. Patterson, Bob, and Joe stopped by my office." Given the fact that Dr. Patterson is the most prominent figure out of the group, it is perfectly natural (and the unfortunate lot of administrators everywhere) for these others to remain unmentioned.

When it comes to the women at the empty tomb, clearly Mary Magdalene is the most prominent figure, and so anyone reporting these details would mention her, but, depending on their purposes, they may or may not mention the others. This resolves any tension across these parallel accounts.

Did the women tell the others or not?

In Mark's Gospel, the women left the empty tomb, and "they said nothing to anyone, for they were afraid" (Mark 16:8). Matthew's Gospel, on the other hand, pictures it this way: "And they departed quickly from the tomb with fear and great joy and ran to report it to His disciples" (Matt. 28:8).[25] Again, there is no question that these reports are different. The question, then, is whether these reports can be reconciled.

And they most certainly can. What most likely is happening here is that, in the Matthew passage, the women return from the tomb scared and keep silent for a while (which is what Mark describes). After some time has passed, however, then they run to the disciples and report their experience with great joy. We notice in the Matthew passage the allusion to their having a feeling of "fear and great joy." So perhaps they had to work out these competing emotions for a brief time before the joy impelled them to speak with the disciples. If so, the problem is solved.

Differences and reliability

Rather than casting doubt on these accounts, these sorts of (compatible) differences of detail actually provide reason to think that the accounts are reliable. If two accounts are supposed to be independent (that is, not relying on each other), then they *should not* be identical in the details they emphasize. This is because, when describing a typical event, it is virtu-

---

25   John and Luke similarly say that the women reported to the disciples what they had seen.

ally impossible for two witnesses to employ the very same details in their descriptions. What we should expect with eyewitness testimony is discrepancies. It is a problem when these discrepancies are irreconcilable, but it is actually a boon to their authenticity when they paint a fuller yet consistent picture.

J. Warner Wallace, a cold case detective turned apologist, has said:

> If there's one thing my experience as a detective has revealed, it's that witnesses often make conflicting and inconsistent statements when describing what they saw at a crime scene. They frequently disagree with one another and either fail to see something obvious or describe the same event in a number of conflicting ways. The more witnesses involved in a case, the more likely there will be points of disagreement.[26]

Wallace goes on to say that the disagreement is often due to someone representing a different but valuable perspective or vantage point. Coming to understand these different perspectives speaks volumes about what is going on in the event being described.

So far, all I have pointed out is alternate ways of understanding certain passages that, if right, resolve apparent tensions. But how do I know the reconciled reading is the correct one? Something to notice is that a critic of the Bible will almost always approach Scripture as if the mere possibility of contradiction means that there is a contradiction. That is, any sign of difference will go down on the long list of alleged Bible contradictions. This, however, is simply uncharitable and a standard to which we don't typically hold people. Moreover, we should remember that the claim is not that these accounts are *possibly* contradictory, but they that they are *indeed* contradictory. In response to this objection, if we can show that there is a reading that resolves the apparent tension, then the charge of contradiction is blocked. It is my experience that the allegation of contradiction quickly fades away by simply looking carefully at the passages.

We've looked at two objections to Christianity that I think are not too

---

26 J. Warner Wallace *Cold Case Christianity: A Homicide Detective Investigates the Claims of the Gospels* (Colorado Springs, CO: David C. Cook, 2013), 74.

difficult to handle. This is not to say these are not worth our time, but just that explanations are typically forthcoming without too much difficulty. We turn now to an objection to the very existence of God: the problem of evil. In my view, the problem of evil requires considerably greater effort to adequately address. I believe Christianity has the resources to address the problem, but it is one that takes greater care.

The Problem of Evil

There's a lot of pain and suffering in the world from which it seems no one is completely immune. It only takes a moment to think of the last heart-wrenching tragedy to which the media-machine has forced our undivided attention. And for some of us, the pain and suffering is right there in our midst. The existence of pervasive pain and suffering in the world has long been a challenge for belief in God.

It is not, however, a problem for all views of God. Pain and suffering, along with the actions and events most of us will label as "evil," are problems only when the theist thinks God is all-powerful and wholly good. If, for example, one thinks that God is sometimes evil, then of course evil wouldn't be a problem for this conception of God. The evil in the world, in this view, is not a problem, but this unfortunately comes at the great cost of one of God's perfections, which amounts to denying the Christian God.

So here's the problem: if God is all-powerful, then he should be able to bring about a world where there is no evil. If God is perfectly good, then he should want to bring about a world where there is no evil. But there is evil. So, the claim is that the existence of an all-powerful and perfectly good God (God* hereafter) is logically incompatible with the existence of evil in the world. In argument form:

1. If God* exists, then there is no evil.

2. There is evil.[27]

3. Therefore, God★ does not exist.

It is worth noting that some religions do, in fact, deny the existence of pain and suffering (that is, they deny premise 2) and say that it is merely an illusion. This is hard to take seriously, and I imagine it would be a hard sell for most grief counselors (and hopefully not something your anesthesiologist believes!). So denying premise 2, it seems to me, is not an option. Thus, the entire case here hinges on whether there is good reason for believing or rejecting premise 1.

There was a time when this argument was taken by the broader philosophical community to be a knock-down-drag-out argument against the existence of God★. But there has been a complete reversal on this (which almost never happens in philosophy, by the way), where even many atheists will admit that the argument is no good, at least as stated. The reason is that it is too strong. Premise 1 asserts that God★'s existence is logically incompatible with the existence of any evil (or pain and suffering) at all. All it would take to defeat premise 1 is one instance of evil that God★ would be justified in allowing. An all-powerful and good God could allow pain and suffering so long as this were the means to achieve a greater good that was only achievable through allowing the evil.

What has convinced many thinkers is that free choice is a good that is only achievable by allowing for the possibility of evil. This is referred to as the *free will defense*. Let's suppose Tom has himself a girlfriend named Susie. Let's also suppose that things are going really well for Tom and Susie, until he finds out that Susie is being paid off by his parents to date him. The whole thing, he comes to conclude, is a fraud. Isn't it of a far greater value for Tom to be with someone who *freely chooses* to love him? But notice that if there is freedom of choice, there is the possibility of being rejected.

---

27 Many theists point out that the atheist cannot affirm premise 2 since, if they do not believe in God, there is no good or evil. An atheist has to say that good and evil are either nothing more than useful fictions or are reducible to something like pleasure and pain, respectively. But in both of these options, evil does not really exist. I do think that the atheist has a problem here, but the argument can be made by recasting the problem in terms of pain and suffering. The thought would be that an all-powerful and good God would be able to and want to eradicate all pain and suffering. To create a world with pervasive pain and suffering seems morally wrong, and thus there cannot be a good God, or so the argument goes.

Likewise, God could have created individuals who were constrained to robotically sing his praises and follow his wishes all the day long, but free worship is arguably of greater worth. Notice, however, that free creatures do not *have to* choose to worship or follow the dictates of God; otherwise they wouldn't be free. So, if God creates free creatures, then He allows for the possibility that these creatures will choose the wrong. But if free and genuine worship is of a far greater value than robotic and forced worship (if forced actions can even count as worship), then creating creatures who would freely worship justifies allowing for at least some evil. Thus, premise 1 is shown to be untrue. It is not the case that if God★ exists, there can be no evil, because the possibility of evil had to exist in order for God★ to achieve the good of free worshippers.

The overall rejoinder to someone who is raising this version of the problem of evil is that, so long as it is even possible that God has a morally sufficient reason for allowing evil, then the existence of evil is not a logical problem for God's existence.

A more difficult version of the problem of evil is to argue that it is not so much that if God★ exists, there should be no evil at all, but to make a point about how much and how vicious the evil is that we see in the world. In this version, the claim is that there is at least some evil for which God does not have a justifying reason. It is not the mere existence of evil, but the existence of unjustified evil that may seem to cast doubt on the existence of an all-powerful and all-good God. Here the argument can be formulated as:

4. If God★ exists, then there is no unjustified evil.

5. There is unjustified evil.

6. Therefore, God★ does not exist.

I don't have the space to give a full treatment to this argument, but let me indicate some of the directions that hold great promise.

This time it is premise 5 that is controversial, because it is difficult to see how God★ could sit idly by in allowing evil for which he has no justifying purpose. Surely, it is thought, an all-good God would not allow evil to occur for no reason at all. So, premise 4, for many theists, looks to be true.

The argument here turns on whether one thinks there is unjustified evil or not.[28]

One important response is to say that we are not in a position to know that premise 5 is true. The reason for this is that we occupy a very limited perspective from a tiny slice of history. We can barely discern the intentions of people we know extremely well (especially when we are married to them!), and they are finite. So how could we know whether God, who knows the end from the beginning, allowed certain events for good reasons? We are simply not in a position to say that God wouldn't have justification in allowing these.

This seems to create something of a stalemate. The atheist cannot give any compelling reasons for premise 5. But do we have reason to deny it? We *do*, and we have already presented some of these reasons in this book. The reason we have to think that there is no unjustified evil is because there is reason to believe that God★ exists in the first place. If we have reason to think God★ exists, and we agree that if God★ exists, there is no unjustified evil, well, then, it follows that there is no unjustified evil. In argument form:

7. If God★ exists, then there is no unjustified evil.

8. God★ exists.

9. Therefore, there is no unjustified evil.

Notice how we've changed the argument. Remember that we all agree on what is now premise 7. The theist asserts premise 8 and supports it with the many arguments for God's existence. What follows is that there is no unjustified evil, and, thus, premise 5 above is false.

What is nice about this is that it puts into sharp relief the stakes of the argument. One either thinks God★ exists or one thinks unjustified evil exists. When put like this, I think we see that the Christian theist is on good ground, because there are really compelling reasons to think that God★ exists and a real lack of reasons for thinking that unjustified evil exists.

---

28 Sometimes the argument is cast even more modestly:
    1.   If God★ exists, then there is no unjustified evil.
    2.   There is probably unjustified evil.
    3.   Therefore, God★ probably does not exist.
Though the argument is more modest, it still hinges on reasons for thinking there is unjustified evil.

What a lot of people seem to find difficult with God and evil is that it seems like it would be so easy for God to decrease the suffering in the world, given his omnipotence. There are at least two responses for why this is misguided.

First, this idea suggests that the point of life is for us to be happy and pain-free. But this is not the case. God didn't create us merely so we could be pleased in life. In the Christian view, God created us to know and bring glory to him, so the quantity of pain in the world is not obviously in tension with this end in the same way that it would be if God primarily wanted us to be pleased.

Secondly, we can't separate God's omnipotence from his omniscience. God, being omniscient, literally knows all truths—not just what the case is but also what the case would be if things were different. So, could God have prevented lots of evils, like the Holocaust, given his omnipotence? Sure, but given his omniscience, perhaps he knew there would have been far worse evils as a result. By contrast, we, given our finitude, are simply not in a position to know what would happen if God had limited some moral or natural evil. It is easy to say that if we had God's omnipotence, we would make the world a far better place. But this is irrelevant unless we also had God's omniscience and knew the far-reaching results of our actions.

The Hiddenness of God

It is sometimes asserted that God, if he exists, is not obvious. Some atheists say they would happily believe in God if (and really only if) God made himself directly evident to them. The thinking is that it should be no problem for God, being all-powerful, to make himself known in such a way that people will be more compelled to believe in him. This gives us the argument for divine hiddenness:

1. If God★ existed, then God★ would make his existence more obvious.

2. God★ is not obvious.

3. Therefore, God★ does not exist.

In addressing this challenge, I think we should agree with the atheist that, at least in a certain respect, God could be more obvious in revealing himself. I'm not sure about you, but God has never gotten my attention via a burning bush, as he did with Moses, and Jesus never blinded my eyes to make his point that he is who he claimed to be, as he did Saul of Tarsus. God clearly has the ability to rend such events actual in all of our lives, and if he did, he would be more obvious. Most people in the history of the world have not had their lives interrupted by an extraordinary and manifest appearance of God, and thus God is, to some degree, veiled.

Now this is a limited concession, since I also think that there is a real and obvious sense in which God makes his existence abundantly clear to all people. In fact, God has created the world replete with revelation of himself that can, as Paul says, be "clearly seen" in creation (Rom. 1:20). This is largely the argument of chapter 3. He is there and can be seen by all.

The complaint seems to be that since God *could* be more obvious (which I am conceding), he *should* be more obvious (which I will be taking to task presently). But why think God is obligated to make himself more obvious than he already has? The only way this is a genuine problem is if God's ability to make himself more obvious morally obligates him to do so. This is something for which proponents of this problem rarely argue. We might wish or prefer that God would be more obvious, but nothing interesting follows logically from unmet wishes or desires.

Do we have reason to think that God *lacks* this obligation? So long as one thinks humans are imperfect, I see no reason to think that God is obligated to make himself more obvious to us. In my view, we all, at a certain point, transgress the moral law that is written on our hearts. If this is our moral condition and God is a holy judge, then it seems to me that God has no obligation to make himself known at all, much less obvious in any kind of extraordinary way.

Furthermore, I think it is a mistake to believe that some display from God would really make all the difference in the world for most people. I once heard a prominent atheist say on national television that he wouldn't believe in God even if God himself spoke verbally to him. He would instead check himself into a mental hospital because, obviously, he is hearing voices, and we have treatments for that. What this atheist got right is that experiences can be very powerful, but the utility of an experience largely has to do with how we interpret it. Without the proper lens of interpretation, miraculous events are only marginally helpful for bringing about the sort of response that God seeks.

If we are honest, we all want some special effects to accompany our dealings with God. The problem is that these elements often distract us from seeing our sin and even distract us from seeing God himself. The nation of Israel witnessed many supernatural events throughout its history. Many times, the miraculous events did not bring about the sort of life change one would expect (see in Numbers 13-14, for example, the generation of Israelites who were part of the exodus from Egypt but in the end failed to trust God). Jesus also provided many miracles but was often selective as to when he would perform them. There were many contexts where these supernatural events were not going to produce the sort of faith and humbleness of heart that Jesus sought. People had a tendency to seek the miracles themselves, as if they were some sort of parlor trick, rather than see them as pointing to a further reality—the reality of our need for God.

God could, to be sure, cow all of us into frightful submission. If this is what God wanted, I think it is safe to say that he, being an all-powerful being, could bring this result about, and we should shudder at the possibility. But God is good. He is not interested in your frightful submission. He's also not interested in your devotion only for what you get out of it (parlor tricks, eternal paradise, or whatever else). God is interested in a humble heart that responds in worship to his greatness and goodness. If God is after this specific heart response, then it may be that God's degree of obviousness is perfectly calibrated with the accomplishment of this sort of response.

6

Apologetics and Evangelism

Apologists and evangelists are sometimes at odds. Evangelists sometimes think apologists are overly concerned with giving arguments that may delay indefinitely the sharing of the Gospel. Apologists sometimes think evangelists do not take answering honest questions seriously enough.

Unfortunately, for some, this is not too far from the truth. Some apologists seem more concerned about arguing than they do about sharing the Gospel, and some evangelists tend to make light of certain deep questions. But while there are excesses on both sides, I will argue that evangelism and apologetics, when done properly, are not mutually exclusive pursuits. In fact, they fit together so naturally when engaging unbelievers that it is often difficult to discern when one is doing apologetics and when one is doing evangelism. This, it seems to me, is precisely how it should be.

I think the primary mistake here is thinking that there are so-called apologists and evangelists, as if one must choose between these two options. This isn't to say these aren't distinct disciplines. We'll be sure to make the distinctions in a moment. However, as disciples of the Lord Jesus, we are commanded to love God with all of who we are (Matt. 22:37-38). We are also commissioned to go make disciples (Matt. 28:19-20) who will also love God with all of who they are. This is going to take both evangelism and apologetics, as well as other disciplines. To characterize people as either apologists or evangelists is to parse this commission in a way that is unsupported by the text. In my view, any apologist who doesn't see the relevance of the Gospel has lost sight of the whole point for doing apologetics. Also, any evangelist who merely presents the Gospel and declines answering any questions, shaking the proverbial dust from his/her proverbial sandals, is forsaking a biblical call on his/her life.

Okay, now for the distinctions. I think the distinction between apologetics and evangelism is best made in terms of the specific aims of each discipline, though, as we'll see, these are clearly related. Evangelism aims to present the good news of the Gospel to an unbeliever and calls that person to repentance and faith in Jesus Christ as the initial phase of the commission to make disciples. Apologetics has the task of commending (providing positive reason to believe) and defending (addressing questions and objections to) the truth claims of Christianity without making any Christian assumptions.

Occasionally, it is objected that no one gets saved as result of apologetic discussion. Is this right? In one sense, I actually agree that no one gets saved as a result of apologetic discussion. But this is because the work of apologetics is *pre-evangelistic*. No one gets saved because getting saved is not the goal of apologetics. That is, the goal of apologetics is intellectual assent and a general openness to the Gospel. As stated above, the goal in apologetics is to commend and defend the truth claims of Christianity. However, (and this is really important) *merely coming to believe that Christianity is true is not the same as placing one's faith in Christ.* Intellectual assent is obviously an important step in the journey, but it is not salvific. James reminds us that even the demons believe (James 2:19)! Indeed, our churches, especially here in the Bible Belt, are filled with people who agree with much of the teaching. Just think of the folks who come to church on Christmas and Easter and may even believe that Jesus was born of a virgin and rose from the dead. The problem is that these folks have never placed their faith in Jesus Christ and his work on the cross. No amount of apologetics is going to address their need for faith. In a word, they need to be evangelized.

The goal of apologetics is intellectual assent and a general openness to the Gospel. Now, notice that this goal links apologetics inextricably to the evangelistic task. Once there is some degree of assent or openness to the Gospel, then it is our duty to share Christ.

Does evangelism always involve apologetics?

There's no doubt that there are times in which a simple Gospel presentation is all that is needed for a person to come to faith. There was a time in our country when our culture was predominantly Christian-influenced, and even if a person had never made a decision for Christ, he/she had still likely absorbed something of a Judeo-Christian worldview. When the Holy Spirit brings conviction for someone like this, often all that is needed is a simple Gospel presentation.

However, by all accounts, our country and culture are trending away from their Christian influence. Now, I believe that the Holy Spirit can still bring conviction from a straightforward Gospel presentation anytime he so chooses. However, in many cases, people do not even have the basic categories to grasp the content of the Gospel because of their lack of Christian background. More and more, there's a need for the equivalent of what Bible translators do for an unreached people group. The Bible translator must get the content of the Gospel into the vernacular of the people for an individual to even grasp that content. Could the Holy Spirit miraculously allow the tribesman to understand the Gospel in a foreign language? Absolutely. However, it often takes the hard work of translation. Likewise, God can bring conviction if he wants to, but it often takes the hard work of engaging in apologetic discussion for someone to be able to grasp the content of the Gospel, especially in so-called blue states and secular college campuses.

What also complicates things is the string of best-selling books written by atheists with the express purpose of "converting" people to atheism. There are millions of people reading these books and being influenced by them. Many of the challenges are rhetorically powerful, and this movement of New Atheism is growing steadily. As we mentioned in chapter 2, though the challenges are rhetorically powerful, they are, somewhat ironically, rather weak philosophically. We have the amazing opportunity to respond to these weak challenges and, I think, soundly address them. But a mere Gospel presentation in the face of attack often falls on deaf ears with this group. It is going to take winsomely but forcefully demolishing these arguments and ideas that are set up against the knowledge of God (2 Cor. 10:5).

But let me stress that we have to get to the Gospel. It is not our job to argue someone up to the steps of the Kingdom before sharing the Gospel. We should be agile enough to move into an apologetics discussion, and as we are able to address someone's questions, we should then move into an evangelistic mode. But perhaps, in the midst of evangelizing, we hit upon another question that seems to stand in front of faith. As we address this new question, we must look once again to share the Gospel. And remember, in all of this, it is all about being faithful to Christ.

Doing Evangelism and Apologetics

We turn now to look at some great examples of how evangelism and apologetics work together. Let's first look at a biblical example: Paul in Athens (Acts 17:16-34).

Paul's interactions in Athens are often cited for their apologetic import. However, there is much controversy as to just how much apologetic value we can glean. What seems clear is that, at points, Paul is making a defense, but it is also clear that he is keeping his eye on the prize such that the defense is in service of the Gospel.

Paul begins his speech with a compliment.

> So Paul stood in the midst of the Areopagus and said, "Men of Athens, I observe that you are very religious in all respects." (v. 22)

The men of Athens are highly religious, but Paul is going to suggest that there is perhaps one God they do not yet know. Paul begins to describe one who is not among the gods of the Greek or Roman pantheon. This is a being far greater than Zeus or Apollo. The very existence of all things in reality literally depends upon him. This is the true God whom they have been seeking with all of this religious fervor. He says:

> For while I was passing through and examining the objects of your worship, I also found an altar with this inscription, 'TO AN UNKNOWN GOD.' Therefore what you worship in ignorance, this I proclaim to you. The God who made the world and all things in it, since He is Lord of heaven and earth, does not dwell in temples made with hands; nor is He served by human hands, as though He

needed anything, since He Himself gives to all people life
and breath and all things; and He made from one man
every nation of mankind to live on all the face of the earth,
having determined their appointed times and the bound-
aries of their habitation, that they would seek God, if perhaps they might grope for Him and find Him, though He
is not far from each one of us; for in Him we live and
move and exist, as even some of your own poets have said,
'For we also are His children.' (v. 23-28)

Notice that Paul quotes some of their poets. There are also allusions to
the philosophical ideas at home in the group to whom he is speaking. We
should also notice that Paul does not reason with them from the Scriptures, as he often did with the Jews. This is because the Greeks with whom
he was speaking would not have taken Scripture as truth, and to reason
with them from that vantage point would not have been effective. Instead,
he spoke the vernacular of the people. He showed them that even their
own philosophical tradition was looking for the true God.

Here comes the argument:

> Being then the children of God, we ought not to think that
> the Divine Nature is like gold or silver or stone, an image
> formed by the art and thought of man. Therefore having
> overlooked the times of ignorance, God is now declaring
> to men that all *people* everywhere should repent. (v. 29-30)

Even the Athenian poet says that we are his children. If we are like God,
then God could not merely be made of gold or silver or stone fashioned by
mankind. He is far greater than all this because we are greater than these.
Thus, God is an authority, and one to whom we should submit. Why?

> ... because He has fixed a day in which He will judge
> the world in righteousness through a Man whom He has
> appointed, having furnished proof to all men by raising
> Him from the dead. (v. 31)

Paul masterfully brings the apologetic conversation to Christ's work on
the cross. He speaks in the vernacular of his audience, shows he is adept at

their own philosophical thought, and proceeds to use that to point directly at their need for Christ. Unfortunately, the brilliance of the presentation is not well-received. They revert to the tactics of many who are presented with a truth that they cannot outwit.

> Now when they heard of the resurrection of the dead, some began to sneer, but others said, "We shall hear you again concerning this." So Paul went out of their midst. (v. 32-33)

Did Paul fail? Some have charged that Paul abandoned apologetics because of the paltry results in Athens. However, we can only read such a thing into the passage. And moreover, some do, in fact, believe:

> But some men joined him and believed, among whom also were Dionysius the Areopagite and a woman named Damaris and others with them. (v. 34)

The reality is that Paul was successful because he was a faithful witness.

A personal example

It is often the case that people have certain issues that seem to block them from having faith. They may think there are certain objections that cannot be satisfactorily answered. Or they may think that all Christians are bigots who foster hate and violence. We all bring certain baggage and bias into almost every discussion. Addressing these biases and attempting to divest someone of their baggage that doesn't track with the truth can be a very important moment for someone coming to faith.

I remember a young couple for whom I had been praying for quite some time. He was from Malaysia, she was from Japan, and they were living together, having met and fallen in love at school. The woman had a significant block to her faith that made it difficult for her to believe. The blockage was that her father had tragically passed away years earlier. The difficulty was that coming to faith was, for her, tantamount to saying that her father was in hell, since he died an unbeliever. Though the Gospel is good news, it did not sound like good news for her.

I could have presented the Gospel, and if they didn't respond, I could have simply walked away. However, I couldn't responsibly do this. They were definitely searching, but they had this intellectual issue, and they needed help for how to think about it. The situation called for an apologetic discussion.

I pointed out that, sadly, truth is not always pleasant. I don't *like* the fact that anyone's eternal destination is hell. But a mere feeling of aversion toward something isn't a good reason to disbelieve it. I often don't like the experience of seeing the balance of my checking account at the bank. I sometimes wish it had a few more zeroes added to the backside of it. But my aversion to this would be a terrible reason to go on a shopping splurge, denying the reality that is my checking account. Of course, this is nowhere near the level of the sort of thoughts this young couple needed to process. But nonetheless, the point remains that we cannot pick and choose what we like and do not like about reality and expect that to change reality. If something turns out to be true, then we should accept it, no matter how unpleasant it is. I told them that what they needed to do was consider whether or not the Gospel is true. If it turns out to be false, then there's no big deal. However, if it is true, then it would be far worse to simply ignore this reality, no matter how unpleasant. With this intellectual hurdle cleared out of the way, they eventually came to faith and are involved in ministry to this day.

The point is that in order to do effective evangelism, especially in our current post-Christian age, we ought to be equipped with apologetics.

How to effectively use apologetics in evangelistic situations

The most important tool in knowing how to do apologetically minded evangelism is asking good questions.

Some people might say:

"I can't believe in Christianity because there is too much pain and suffering in the world."

I don't suggest launching immediately into a sermon on solving the problem of evil (discussed in chapter 5). When we do this, defensive walls immediately go up, and very little is heard. Instead, I suggest having a genuine discussion. One way to initiate a discussion is to ask the following question:

"Why do you think pain and suffering is a problem for believing in God?"

It has been my experience that, in most cases, a person will not be able to articulate what the exact problem is. You may need to supply some content here (remember that you have approached apologetics devotionally and have worked through these issues already, right?), and then you can begin to talk about how you go about resolving this difficulty. The point is that engaging in a shouting match—with them saying, "Evil's a problem," and you saying, "No it isn't"—is not going to be a fruitful approach.

Let's say they claim:

"There is too much evil in the world for God to have a justifying reason for all of it."

I would suggest responding with another thoughtful question:

"How do you know what God's justifying reasons are?"

Asking them strategic questions does two things. First, it validates them as a person, but second, it pushes them to support their position.

It validates them by inviting them into a dialogue rather than forcing them to listen to your monologue. You become peers engaged as dialogue partners, both presumably in search of the truth. Asking good questions shows your interlocutors that you are interested in what they have to say.

But it also pushes them to support their position. It's easy to throw out a claim, but it is much more difficult to substantiate a claim. Our current political scene sometimes feels devoid of any thoughtfulness precisely because candidates and pundits are forced to make their case (or respond to challenges) within sound bites, often with no more than 140 characters. In such a reality, value is not placed on truth; instead, it is given to whoever is able to make the snappiest quip.

Asking a question about the problem of evil forces people to support their quips. And as we've seen, atheists are not in the strongest position when it comes to the supporting the idea that God couldn't have justifying reasons for the pain and suffering in the world. You could point this out to them.

But it is far more effective to ask questions that lead them to reveal the weakness in their argument themselves.

What will happen occasionally is that you will encounter someone who has thought through these sorts of questions already and has well-thought-out responses. Along the way, you will undoubtedly find yourself in a position where you don't know how to answer certain charges. In this case, you should admit that you do not know but promise to find out and get back with the person. This shows humility and honesty, and I think it goes much further than pretending we have an answer when we do not. Saying "I don't know" keeps the discussion a dialogue in the pursuit of truth. When we merely pretend to know something, we typically lose our credibility. It is really important, though, that, whenever possible, we do not forsake the opportunity to continue this conversation once we've had the opportunity to search out answers. Some of the greatest teaching moments for me have been times when I felt like I had failed in making a good defense. These are moments in which I felt driven to discover answers to the questions on which I misfired.

When it comes to unbelievers, the important thing is to be ready to give a defense with the ultimate aim of sharing the Gospel. So long as we are faithful in this, we can truly leave the results up to God.

APPENDIX 1
COLLEGE GUIDE

Here's the reality of our typical secular college campuses: our Christian kids are getting eaten alive! This may sound overly dramatic, but it has become increasingly difficult to be an evangelical Christian in your typical institution of higher learning.

Why is this?

By all accounts, there is a much greater concentration of atheists among college professors than in the general public. And the percentage of evangelicals working in the academy is even more disproportionate. On the level of worldview, many Christian kids are out of place and represent a *worldview minority*.[29] I would describe the typical university setting as a place that is not specifically favorable toward Christian faith, and there are growing pockets of extreme hostility.

Now, I must say that these pockets can sometimes be a bit exaggerated. We can sometimes get the picture that all secular philosophy professors are attempting to disabuse their students of their faith. Though this definitely happens, on behalf of many of my philosophy professor friends who are atheists, let me say that I don't think this is the majority. My atheist friends who teach philosophy will not let pat answers and philosophically simple views go unchallenged, but a student choosing to be a Christian theist in a reasonable way is no problem for many of the professors I know. Of course, there are exceptions to this. There are professors—found not just

---

29 I'd be the first to admit that this is not the exact same situation as being a minority as it relates to race. These are sociologically different in terms of specific features of the experience. However, some of the feelings of isolation can be analogous.

in philosophy but also in the hard and soft sciences and other disciplines as well—who are very hostile toward Christian faith.

But the odd professor who is an angry atheist is not what causes most students to walk away from their faith.

Where students face much greater hostility is when it comes to social issues. A student can be a vocal socialist, a communist, or an anarchist. One can deny that we have any knowledge of reality at all or even think that science is just a power play. You may hear professors and students assert that animals deserve the same rights as humans, and many (if not most) professors think that unborn infants may be terminated. You'll even find a few who think that even newborn infants may be terminated up to a certain point. With regards to sexual ethics, there is a blinding variety of courses pertaining to just about every sexual issue you can imagine, including classes on pornography and the celebration of "Sex Week" that occurs with university funding on many campuses across the country. This isn't to say that these are all majority views on the college campus, but they are all acceptable views for people to hold. However, if you defend traditional marriage, even with subtle distinctions and clear arguments, you will be labeled a bigot and an unintelligent nut.

What causes Christian young people to stumble is that it can be difficult to bear the oppressive weight of this secular environment. It can, at times, be oppressive in at least two ways. The first is the intellectual pressure of being in this environment. Again, a large majority of professors are not overtly hostile, but the Christian student is nevertheless in the minority, and the student's religious faith does not fit in. The student has to be constantly on-guard and careful to filter the ideas that are being peddled in the classroom. Sometimes the pressure to fit in intellectually can be overwhelming.

The second social pressure is a moral pressure, and this, I think, actually feeds into the first pressure, as I'll explain below. Let's face it: most people who fall away from the Christian faith do not do so because of a lack of apologetic training. The reality is that most people who leave the faith do so because they simply want to live their lives as if there is no God—that is, as if there are no moral constraints. Think about it. A typical public college is chock-full of 18- to 24-year-olds who, perhaps for the first time in their lives, get to decide how they live their lives, without mom, dad, pastor, or youth pastor keeping them in check. They can, in many cases, drink alcohol, do recreational drugs, and have sex basically at will, often without any consequences whatsoever (or, at least, so they think).

We'd be fools to think this isn't an incredible attraction to typical students, even when they come from a Christian background. The only thing standing in the way of what looks like a party for the ages is their Christian conscience (i.e., the potential guilt that will come if they drink, smoke, or hook up). So then, the students who are under tremendous social pressure from this environment find themselves in a science philosophy class where their Christian commitments are being challenged. The students now have a way to take care of their Christian conscience: drop the Christian worldview, and they can live however they want.

We all do this, to a certain extent. We allow our moral desires to guide our rational commitments. That is, when we want to behave in a certain way, we will subtly and often unconsciously find a worldview that endorses this behavior. This is why a husband who wants to leave his wife and kids to follow "love" elsewhere or someone who is struggling with same-sex attraction will somehow find these views in Scripture. Is it because those views are really there in Scripture? No, it isn't. These views are not there. But misinterpreting certain passages in such a way that these views seem to be supported by Scripture allows people to adopt these lifestyles. So the student who can't seem to resist the social pressures will begin to find the secular worldview much more attractive.

Should a Christian kid go to a secular institution?

Based on all of this information, you might expect me to say that Christian kids should not go to secular institutions. It may, therefore, surprise you that I think we need to be sending our kids to secular institutions. The reality is that students who choose to go to Christian institutions also face challenges, though perhaps of a different sort. I've unfortunately seen many Christian kids struggle in Christian contexts too, and it is not rare enough that a student can even lose his or her faith in a Christian setting. Sometimes students actually fare better in the secular setting because it forces them to be on-guard, and this helps the students' faith stay strong and genuine.

However, I would only recommend going into a secular institution with eyes wide open, prepared for the challenges one will likely face. I'm convinced that we must redeem college campuses, and this is not going to happen if we avoid them. Also, there are some who are called to achieve at the highest levels of academics and will need to go to top institutions to do this.

Succeeding at a secular institution

This is a really important decision. Indeed, where one goes to college ranks high on the list of life's most important decisions (it's at least in the top ten!). Choosing to go to a secular institution should be done VERY cautiously, but I think a Christian student can succeed.

Here are three suggestions for succeeding on a secular college campus.

First, the student must be connected to a vital Christian community. This is absolutely crucial. Ideally, this would be a local church where one finds good, solid Bible teaching, a vibrant service of worship, and opportunities to engage in ministry. In addition to this, there are a variety of college ministries on most college campuses across the country that exist for the express purpose of helping students succeed as Christians amidst secular social pressures. Many students credit a Christian student group as crucial to their navigating the pressures of college as Christians.

Second, for students to be successful, they should embrace a commitment to the life of the mind as a Christian. That is, students need to approach every issue Christianly and employ the ideas presented in this book. College students have to be on-guard with every idea that comes at them. Many of the ideas will be somewhat neutral (e.g., Caesar crossed the Rubicon in 49 B.C.), but then others will not be (e.g., all biological life has a common ancestor). The student needs to be ready to confront ideas that are antithetical to the Christian worldview. The most important thing for approaching things Christianly is to maintain an active and consistent study of Scripture and theology. Students will also need to be able to think critically about the ideas that will be presented and bring Scripture to bear on these issues in an intelligent way. I would also recommend beginning to amass Christian intellectual heroes, especially, whenever possible, in the field in which the student is studying.

What is not an option, if the student is to be successful, is to act like a sponge in this setting. Christianity is a complete worldview. It cannot merely be what we do on Sunday mornings. If it is merely what students do on Sunday mornings, then eventually they will start sleeping in. Christianity is relevant and broadly informs every area of life.

Third, students need to be involved in ministry. We need Christians to see their universities as a mission field. Indeed, it may, at times, feel like you live among an unreached people group. Again, I think this kind of ministry is best done through a local church, but the campus group may be a great outlet for ministry as well. It is important to initiate this early on, as it is always more difficult to try to begin these things midstream. The wonderful thing about being on a secular campus is that there is no shortage of unbelievers, and there are ample opportunities to make a difference for Christ.

The fact is we need Christians working in the academy. What is said in the university has a profound impact on our culture. We are currently radically underrepresented in most disciplines. There is beginning to be a good representation of Christian philosophers at top research universities. But I'm sad to say that this is the only exception of which I am aware.

Two great callings in going to college

In my view, there are two great callings in going to college. The first one is being called to go to the secular academy in the way that I described above. Some students, however, are called to a Christian setting. This is not because they would otherwise struggle with doubts and perhaps lose their faith. Instead, they are called to be analogous to Special Forces, trained at the highest level of Christian intellectual thought. These will need to learn how to critically evaluate ideas. These will need to be familiar with the major movements of intellectual history, both secular and sacred. These will need to know biblical languages. These will need to know Scripture and theology. These will need opportunities to employ all of this in ministry settings.

I'm quite sure there are places out there engaged in training Special Forces. I know of one such school whose heart beats for this. The College at Southwestern (the undergraduate program at Southwestern Baptist Theological

Seminary) is doing precisely this. In each of our three bachelor's programs, we begin students in their first semester studying the original writings of Homer, Plato, Aristotle, and Cicero. The following semester it is Athanasius, Augustine, Aquinas, and others. This continues every semester up through the late 20th century, where we read Karl Barth, C.S. Lewis, and Jacques Derrida. Students are also trained in the history in which these thinkers worked. There are classes in theology, Bible, and languages. Each student, as a requirement for graduation, must also go on an international mission trip to employ this training in real-life settings. I don't know of an institution with a more innovative program as this for training Special Forces in the ministry.

You can find information about our college program at college.swbts.edu.

APPENDIX 2
HOW TO GET APOLOGETICS AT YOUR CHURCH

How many of you have apologetics or apologetics-related ministries featured at your local church? Unfortunately, it's probably very few. I will briefly lay out a few ways in which we can grow in this area in our churches. Hopefully, I have sufficiently made the case that, with the proper end in view (namely, the Gospel and loving God with our minds), apologetics is a very important area of study and practice. In my view, it will be to our extreme detriment if we do not commit to this lifestyle of *Everyday Apologetics*.

What does this look like on a local church level?

1. Pastors

We are in desperate need of more pastors who will advocate for apologetics. In my experience, many pastors have no specific objection to apologetics, but they do not specifically engage in or support apologetic ministry at the local level. This support can happen in at least two ways. First, the senior pastor should regularly include points within his sermons that have an apologetic thrust in order to prepare his people for challenges that will undoubtedly come. That is, just as there should be, from time to time, a defense of key doctrines and proper principles of interpretation, there must also be a defense of Christianity from challenges that our people face in the world. Again, these challenges are getting more frequent and shriller all the time. Also, as our culture grows more deeply secularized, the DNA of our congregations is changing rapidly. There is little guarantee that people in our congregations have Christian worldviews. As we present the Gospel in Sunday morning worship services, this is more and more going to require a defense of the basic claims of Christianity.

Second, the pastor can support and engage in apologetics through pastoral counseling. It is all too common that people (young or old) have been struggling with some doubts about Christianity but are not taken seriously by their pastors. Instead, they are told to have faith and go pray about it. This, I think, is irresponsible. Now, I definitely think we should pray about all of our struggles, including our doubts. However, some of us are not so constituted to just choose to stop doubting. We need to have our doubts addressed in order to work through them. Listening to what someone is thinking about and walking them through their issues is not, in my view, outside the purview of the pastor's role. It's true that, sometimes, one's doubts can seem, from the outside, to be somewhat trivial. However, they don't feel trivial on the inside of the doubts, and it can be a really important opportunity to explore these matters to come to a surer faith. The tragedy is that people walk away from the faith due to doubts that would be easily answered if we would simply care enough to walk with them through these apologetic issues.

As with everything in the local church, the successful ministries tend to be those that are valued by the senior leadership. We need pastors to have "skin in the game" with apologetics activities.

2. Group life

A second way to involve apologetics on the local church level is to intentionally make apologetic resources available to individuals and small or large group studies. There are a huge number of books on a variety of different apologetic areas, some of which are very accessible. I recommend using these books as a catalyst for discussion within small and large group studies. There are beginning to be more and more apologetic curriculums available as well.[30] I have found that many in the church want to study and discuss these issues but have no idea where to start and how to proceed. A library of resources that individuals and groups can check out would be a great way to serve these needs. People so often go at these matters alone because they think they are the only ones struggling with these questions. We have to build communities where it is safe to ask questions and pursue answers together in dialogue. We forsake a tremendous vehicle for growth if we go at these things alone.

3. Outreach training

Finally, the church should provide actual training for doing apologetics and evangelism. There are many ways to accomplish this. The primary way, in my opinion, is for someone within the congregation to rise up to equip people with apologetics training. For congregations that do not have such a person, there are ways to go outside the church to get this training. A church can host a trained apologist/evangelist to come in for a workshop or even host a small conference. Or a church can take advantage of one of the many great conferences that happen all throughout the year.

If you are in the vicinity of Southwestern Seminary, we have a strong faculty in all the relevant areas of ministry and would love to help train your church. Each spring, we also put on a conference in apologetics—called the Stand Firm conference—with nationally recognized speakers. The conference also features breakout sessions in a variety of different areas relevant to apologetics.

Outreach training falls short if there is no actual outreach. It is absolutely vital for a church to be engaged in reaching the community for Christ. Thus, a wonderful way to emphasize evangelism and apologetics is to go out and actually do evangelism and apologetics within the community. One can learn a lot in an academic classroom, but there's nothing like the classroom of actual experience.

---

30 See sbtexas.com/standfirm for a free online apologetics course that was created mostly by Southwestern Seminary faculty.